What Others Are Saying about This Book . . .

"Any time you feel like quitting, or fear that your dream is beyond your reach, as Tony Volpentest reminds us in his incredibly inspiring book, the only thing holding you back is yourself."

—Dan O'Brien, world and Olympic champion decathlete

"What do the names Lou Ferrigno, Joe DiMaggio, Mary Lou Retton, Tony LaRussa, Vince Lombardi, Rocky Marciano and Mario Andretti have in common? For starters, they are some of the all-time greatest athletes. Tony Volpentest is another name deserving of mention in this list. Years ago, I had the pleasure of presenting Tony with our special achievements award for his dedication and determination to succeed in Paralympic sports and for his commitment to the advancement of physically challenged athletes. Such is his character and commitment that makes him worthy to stand alongside the all-time greats. Tony's book will move, inspire, and challenge you to push yourself no matter the odds!"

—George Randazzo, chairman and founder,
National Italian-American Sports Hall of Fame

"Tony has earned gold medals and an assortment of trophies—but as this story shows, what he's really won is our admiration and respect."

—John Rixley Moore, author of *Hostage of Paradox*

"A heartwarming story about a life filled with purpose, love and worth."

—**Charmaine Hammond, author of** *On Toby's Terms*

"What a story! What a life! A must read!"

—**Leon Logothetis, bestselling author of**
Amazing Adventures of a Nobody

"Are world-class athletes born or made? Tony Volpentest's incredible story shows that no matter where we start the race, we all have it within us to not only catch up with the pack, but pass it and leave it panting in our wake. All it takes is a goal and the unbending will to attain it . . . no matter the obstacles."

—**Oscar Pistorius, "Blade Runner" double amputee world
record holder in the 100, 200 and 400 meters**

"This beautiful book made my heart sing. Tony's remarkable story of triumph reminds us of a universal truth: the human spirit wants to endure."

—**Jennifer Myers, author of** *Trafficking the Good Life*

"This inspirational story should be a recommended read in every school. What a powerful story, what a wonderful role model, for young people everywhere."

—**Chris Cucchiara, author of**
*Lessons from the Gym for Young Adults:
5 Secrets to Being in Control of Your Life*

"If you want to learn how to live life, overcome the obstacles that block your path, you need to read this book. If you open up to it, you will become a better human for having read it."

—**Ron Russell, author of** *Don Carina*

FASTEST MAN IN THE WORLD

The Tony Volpentest Story

TONY VOLPENTEST

BETTIE YOUNGS BOOKS

Disclaimer: This is a true story, and the characters and events are real. However, in some cases, the names, descriptions, and locations have been changed, and some events have been altered, combined, or condensed for storytelling purposes, but the overall chronology is an accurate depiction of the author's experience.

About the Cover: This photo was taken in 1996 during the 100-meter medal ceremony in Atlanta, Georgia. Also pictured are silver medalist Neil Fuller and bronze medalist Bradley Thomas, both from Australia.

Cover photo by *Chris Hamilton Photography*
Cover Design by Tatomir Pitariu
Text Design by Jane Hagaman
Senior Editor: Christine Belleris
About the Author photo of Tony Volpentest by Anne McCarthy,
    One Fine Day Photography
Medal photo: © istockphoto.com/tmarvin

Bettie Youngs Books are distributed worldwide. If you are unable to order this book from your local bookseller, Espresso, or online, you may order directly from the publisher.

BETTIE YOUNGS BOOK PUBLISHERS
www.BettieYoungsBooks.com
info@BettieYoungsBooks.com

ISBN: 978-1-936332-00-7
eBook: 978-1-936332-01-4

Library of Congress Control Number: 2010915366

1. Volpentest, Tony. 2. Olympics. 3. Paralympics. 4. Sports. 5. Track and Field. 6. Family Relationships. 7. Self- image. 8. Self-Confidence. 9. Motivation. 10. Disability. 11. Inspiration.

Printed in the United States of America

Dedication

To my true north, my secret weapon, with you I feel invincible!

Contents

Foreword

by H. Ross Perot

Throughout history, individuals have been remembered for different reasons: some for leadership on the battlefield, in legislative chambers, or at religious institutions; others have been known for their acts of overcoming obstacles and exceeding all expectations. Tony Volpentest is one of those individuals.

Several words come to mind when trying to describe Tony: competitor, conqueror, father, role model, and many others.

When I first heard about Tony, I was truly impressed with his athletic abilities. There are not many world-class athletes and record holders who did not start their sport until high school. To do that and to be born without hands or feet is amazing and inspirational.

With handicaps that have limited others, Tony is an athlete who plays several sports some thought impossible. He excelled in track, won several gold medals, and set world records at the Paralympics. His records were less than one second behind Olympic sprinters who were not wearing prosthetics.

I've had the opportunity to know Tony for more than nineteen years. One quality he has taught me is tenacity. He is a person who has been physically limited all his life, but he is a challenger and fighter. He is a trailblazer and has broken stereotypes.

One of the most important values I hold is the role of loving parents raising their children. Tony was blessed with a family that supported and encouraged him. I believe that is an important quality that has helped him succeed.

Webster's Dictionary defines strength as "the quality or state of being strong: capacity for exertion or endurance." I can think of no better words to characterize Tony.

There's a saying, "You don't know if you can do it, until you try." Not only has Tony tried, but he has succeeded beyond anyone's wildest dreams.

Throughout his life, Tony has lived the words of Winston Churchill: ". . . never give in, never give in, never, never, never . . ."

Acknowledgments

I would like to express my most sincere appreciation and thanks to my wife Kami and my children Alex, John, Kathryn and Karlee for your patience and unwavering love!

I would specifically like to thank my parents, without whom my journey would have never started. Thank you for always guiding me on the right path. My brother Art for your undying love and support! Thanks for taking me under your wing while always allowing me to fly solo when I needed to. Thank you to my family for your years of encouragement, your love and laughs, and for such a powerful sense of family.

To all those who have traveled with me on my journey, especially George Butts and Kathy Whitfield, for your amazing vision and sensitivity on film in regard to my story. From teachers to friends to acquaintances, so many of you gave me strength, others gave me hope, but all have helped grow a vision beyond my own perceived limitations and show how brightly the human spirit can shine!

Heartfelt appreciation and thanks to Ross Perot, the United States Olympic Committee, Shriners Hospitals, St. Pius X School, Edmonds-Woodway High School, the March of Dimes, Sister Isadora, Dr. Daniel Timmons, Dr. David Shurtleff, Dr. Edward Almquist, Dr. Cam Stewart and his wife Jane, Susan Hall, Mark Schone, Michael Moor, Coach Bryan Hoddle, Coach Julie Rowe, Coach Mike Anderson, Robert and Vicki Leasure of Spartan

Training, Mike Pack of Artificial Limb Specialists, Dr. Jason Mulder and Dr. Trevor Ferguson of Adjusted 4 Life Wellness Center, the McAndrew Family, the Simmons Family, Larry Weber, Gail Wood, Joe Hampson, Michael Martinez, Mark Santistevan, Hector Bejarano, Andrew Haws, Rob Miniuk. And of course, all of my sponsors throughout the years.

Last, but not least, a very special thank you to Bettie Youngs of Bettie Youngs Book Publishers. Your total professionalism and persistence in getting my story out never faltered and you kept me motivated and inspired throughout the process. Thank you, as well, to your whole staff and in particular to senior editor Christine Belleris Evans, and to Mark A. Clements for your attention to the details, and to superwoman and publicist Randee Feldman for massaging and nurturing this book with the love and care you have! And to designer Jane Hagaman for the beautiful layout. It has been my honor to work with all of you.

Prologue

The Stares

I walk through the carpeted weight room. Heads turn. I walk through the restaurant. Eyes follow me. I walk through the shopping mall. Heads turn again. Again, and again, and again.

I'm always "on parade," always followed by the stares, the eyes of the strangers who can't stop looking at me but pretend they are looking at something else.

A boy pretends to be looking at a toy, but the pretense is clumsy. He gawks at me while I search for a video game. A man sneaks glances between bites of his dinner at a restaurant. I look in his direction; he lowers his eyes.

All my life I've been followed by the stares. It's impossible for me to blend in with the crowd. I'm anonymous but not unnoticed. Born without hands and feet yet walking confidently under my own power, I am a curiosity. People don't understand what they see.

My arms end above where my wrists should be; my legs at my ankles. One leg is three inches shorter than the other. The odds of being born with all four limbs incomplete is one in a half million. So if the current world population is seven billion, there are only 14,000 of us scattered around the planet.

And so I've come to expect strange and awkward reactions from people when they first meet me. Once I walked into a clothing store, and the sales clerk was startled, unable to avoid the obvious. No hands. No feet. He spoke in an unnecessarily loud voice, as though my lack of extremities had somehow affected my hearing. His gaze darted up and down, then bounced back up to my face as though he did not notice anything unusual.

"May . . . I . . . help . . . you?" he said, each word clearly enunciated and spoken slowly.

I'm missing hands and feet, not a brain, I thought. But I pretended not to notice the clerk's behavior. This is my life; I'm used to it. I imagine that people wonder all kinds of things about me and my life: *How can anyone walk without feet? It must be such a tough thing to live with. How does he manage? What does he use to hold things? Can he get dressed by himself? . . . Can he write? Is he married?* So I try clothes on, I buy clothes, and I walk on, trying to seem oblivious to it all.

Certainly it hasn't been easy. While I never really felt rejected by others, I faced a lifetime of distinctive obstacles. And yet things have turned out quite nicely. Actually, I thank God that I was born like this; it set me on a path that accentuated my strengths, sharpened my focus and resolve, and provided me with the lessons and skills I would use to achieve goals I might otherwise never have thought possible. The love and support of my family, mentors and coaches helped me believe in myself, too, and that has made all the difference.

I became the "fastest man in the world"—without feet. From 1992 to 1999, the records show that no one competing in the leg-amputee portion of the Paralympics had ever run the 100 or 200 meters faster than I. Because of my devotion to training, because of the development of technology that gave me "feet" to run on, because of the support and belief of my parents, I fulfilled a dream of making a living as a professional athlete and becoming one of the highest- paid Paralympic athletes in the world, with a six-figure salary earned through endorsements.

There are good things. Many, actually. One time I was at a restaurant with my girlfriend at the time. People snuck sideways glances at me, as they typically do. When I sat down, a man at a neighboring table leaned over and said, "I know you. You're the guy who runs. I've seen you. Man, you're fast." He put his hand out for a handshake. I extended my arm. We shook. The stares were no longer just looks of disbelief and fear. They were stares of respect and admiration.

It's been an incredible journey, going from the world of "You can't do that" to "How did you ever do so much?"

I've come a long way. Some might find it exceptional but I feel that it's simply living up to my potential. I did what had to be done. Day by day, step by step, I've just been busy living my life.

I've come so far. I have so far to go. This is my story.

Chapter 1

Flying in Formation

Time had slowed to a heartbeat. It was just like in the movies, where you can hear every beat of a butterfly's wings as it lands on a blade of grass, or a drop of sweat trickling until it lands with a "plop" on the pavement. Your senses are so heightened that you can hear not only your own heartbeat but also that of the person next to you.

I focused. Butterflies in my stomach swirled and churned to get out. I took a deep breath and, like I had done so many times before, imagined the butterflies calming to fly in formation. *Breathe in . . . breathe out.* The butterflies settled and started flying together. I focused on my breathing.

But the noise—the cheering, clapping, stomping of thousands of people—drummed in my ears. *Focus . . . breathe . . . focus,* I told myself. Then a sort of tunnel vision overcame me; it was like I was going into a cocoon and everything became silent except for my own breathing and heartbeat.

In a clarifying moment I heard the words of my mother, Betty, ring in my ears. It was the phrase I had heard so many times before, the same ones she uttered on the day I was born. "If there was any doubt about our mission in life, there is no doubt now."

I was snapped out of my reverie by the *pop* of the starting pistol. Adrenaline rushed through my body and up to my head and I catapulted my body forward, forcing my legs to pump ahead with every ounce of strength and energy I had. I still did not hear the screams, the cheers of encouragement. I was utterly focused. Now that I was up and moving, I kept my body low, pushing forward. Because as we all know, a body in motion tends to stay in motion . . . and I wasn't going anywhere but forward as fast as was humanly possible. I felt my torso extend as I transitioned out of my crouch and pushed against the ground beneath me.

Blood pounded in my ears. It was like I was flying ahead, and with every step I emerged further from my tunnel vision. I began to hear the people again. The large crowd was raging. My hearing snapped back as if I had just taken out earplugs. Even as I sensed the tension and expectation around me, I felt my body hit its final gear. There was no stopping me . . . I flew by everyone else, leaving them in my wake.

In an instant it was over.

I wanted to collapse to the ground and cry; at the same time I wanted to wave and smile and laugh and scream. *I did it . . . did what I came to do . . . did what I came to prove.* This was not just a dream—this was real.

For me there has never been a question of my mission in life; I feel I've known it since the day I was born.

The race I'd just run was over, but what had started as a flame burning brightly inside me had just become an inferno, for I had more to prove—and would for the rest of my life.

Chapter 2

My Shocking Beginning

The minutes after my birth were certainly not what my parents—or any parent, for that matter—expected. A mother imagines holding her new baby in her arms and then counting the fingers and toes to make sure they are all there. She is nervous, but not really worried. Of course they'll all be there. They are almost always all there.

That was certainly how it had worked out for my mother and my father, Bill, on five previous occasions. But this time things were different.

My father, Bill, who stood alongside my mother during my delivery, knew something was amiss when the doctor and nurse started speaking together in tense, hushed tones rather than offering congratulations and the traditional announcement of the newborn's sex

My mother knew when the doctor said, "Did you take anything during your pregnancy?" Although I had been born weighing five pounds, two ounces, in the fortieth week of a trouble-free pregnancy, that question could only mean something unexpected, something bad, had happened.

"Doctor," my mother said, "I only took what you told me I could." She strained to see her newborn child.

Meanwhile the staff told Dad to stay by my mother's side. He did so, but still caught a glimpse of me. He blinked hard. Was he hallucinating? He looked again. *The baby has no hands or feet.*

After he recovered from the initial shock, my father's first thought was, *Please let him die.* He hoped that my lungs, heart, or liver hadn't properly developed, so I wouldn't have to live like this. And he had the rest of the family to consider. With five other children to support, taking care of a disabled child would be an all-consuming commitment. It would be overwhelming, it would probably be expensive—and who knew what else? What kinds of health problems would I have? What would happen to me if something bad happened to my parents? But in fact, my condition gave him strength because he said: "I want this child more than I've ever wanted a child."

One thing was certain: Life would not be easy with me around.

What had caused my defects? My mother had only followed the doctor's orders. There was no history of birth defects in either of my parents' backgrounds.

The doctors did not show me to my mother right away. In fact she would not lay eyes on me for twenty-four hours after my birth. She held me for the first time on that rainy October afternoon; "He is so beautiful," she said through tears of joy. "Welcome to the world, Anthony Charles!"

And to father she said, "If there was any doubt about our mission in life, there is no doubt now."

Thank God for my parents. Not only did Mom's pronouncement become a mission—one she and my dad would never renounce—it became one that would produce exciting times and take them on journeys to faraway places for extraordinary events. Because of their son's missing hands and feet, their own lives would be enriched. They would travel the world and be interviewed on national TV, meet fascinating people and have a great deal of fun.

But on the day of my birth, my mother must have been scared, holding this seemingly helpless, deformed child who would undoubtedly have a difficult future.

Back in the early seventies there were no special accommodations for handicapped people. No one in our family and none of our friends or neighbors had ever been afflicted with any disability, never mind something as rare as this.

It was my dad's job that day to tell the rest of the family the staggering news of my birth defect. When he got home, he told his eleven-year-old stepdaughter, Sherry, that her new brother had no hands or feet. She thought it was a cruel joke and burst into tears. My grandparents took the news solemnly. They wondered what would become of me. My maternal grandmother told my mom, "You can deal with this; you will cross this mountain a day at a time."

My birth defect tormented my father. At the time he was a heavy drinker; was that to blame? It pained him to watch me struggle. It pained him to hear the doctor say, "Tony will never walk without prosthetics." It pained him to think I would never play like other children, that I would never live a "normal" life.

My mother, however, had the strength of Gibraltar. Later she told me, "It was my mother who taught me a simple, but important, lesson. In the face of adversity, you do whatever it takes to endure. She taught me to face problems head on. Hiding from them never solved anything. It only makes matters worse."

The day after my birth, my mom asked her doctor two questions:

"Will my baby ever be able to walk?"

"Yes," he said, "but he will need prosthetics."

"Will he be able to attend public school?"

"Yes," he said guardedly, "but he will need special help."

"Those answers were important to me," said my mom. "I wanted my Tony to be as normal as possible. I wanted him to go to school like everyone else."

Within the first few days of my life, my parents got some helpful advice from Dr. David Shurtleff, a pediatrician. He didn't mince words. He suggested "tough love." They'd never heard that term before. Dr. Shurtleff told them about the value of teaching accountability and self-worth. "Always love," he told them, "but never smother them."

For the next several years, Shurtleff guided my parents through the emotional travails of raising a disabled child.

"He prepared us for some of the pitfalls we'd face," my dad said. "Sometimes parents get themselves into the bind of trying to do too much, while feeling it's never enough. Most importantly, he kept us on track."

"Tony can do everything every other kid can do," said Dr. Shurtleff. "Do not let anyone intimidate you into thinking otherwise."

So, with his help, my folks stood their ground. Shurtleff's message was as simple as it was clear. Just because I didn't *look* like everyone else didn't mean I wasn't *like* everybody else—in every other way. From the moment I was born, the single-minded goal was to nurture my independence, allowing me to pursue a normal life.

My mom got the message. She let me ride my bike to the nearby playground, and she let me play basketball in fourth and fifth grades on the school team. She basically pretended I had hands and feet, so I could grow up like a normal kid. But pretending could only go so far.

When I was ten months old, my parents faced a critical and agonizing decision. Should I have experimental surgery on my arms that would allow me to have primitive hands? Or should I wait until new technologies were developed?

The experimental surgery they were considering had never before been performed in the United States, or on a ten-month-old. It had been developed in Germany in 1946, for soldiers whose hands had been blown off by mines or artillery.

The procedure involved separating the ulna and radius bones in the forearm to provide a pincer-like grasping appendage. The *pronator teres* muscles in the arm, which in able-bodied people flexes the elbow and rotates the forearm, are utilized to power the grasp of the pincer. With two "fingers" on each arm, I would have about 85 percent of the function of a normal hand, allowing me to grasp objects. And I would possess the sense of touch, a feature prosthetics could not provide.

Many doctors at University Hospital in Seattle were opposed. They said the procedure would require cutting the growth plates in my arms, which would stunt their development. Others said that prosthetic hooks could be mechanically attached, which would avoid the risk of surgery. Others cautioned that the "pincers," which looked like a lobster claw, would eventually frighten my peers, causing them to shun me even more. To add insult to injury, there would also be horrible-looking scars. And finally, there were no guarantees that the operation would even work. The success of this surgery is dependent on many factors, not the least of which are patient expectations and motivations. Since I was just a baby, the post-surgical outcome was therefore unknown.

Those doctors who advocated for the surgery pointed out that I'd never remember being any other way. What's more, since I was already learning to adapt to living without hands, if the surgery were delayed I'd have to re-adapt later in life, which would be difficult and stressful.

"It wasn't like we were burning bridges," my surgeon, Dr.

Edward Almquist, said. "If Tony later wanted mechanical hands, it could be done any time after surgery."

And so I had the surgery. Insurance refused to pay for the operation because I was not a critical risk health wise, but under Dr. Shurtliff's efforts The March of Dimes did.

Eight months later, I underwent a second operation to remove scar tissue from one arm and to do surgery on the second arm.

Gradually I learned how to use my new hands. Eventually, as a young teenager, I would bowl a 199 on the bowling team, play the piano, type, and beat my siblings in computer games.

"I was wondering how he was going to zip up his pants after he started kindergarten," my mom said. "I thought maybe I could put loops on his zipper or maybe I could put Velcro in his pants and take the zippers out. But he was one step ahead of me."

I figured out how to zip up my pants all by myself.

"Tony was always able to figure out how to do things himself," she said. "That's how he's always been."

When I turned fourteen we visited the Shriners Hospital for Children in Portland, Oregon, which specializes in treating orthopedic and neuromusculoskeletal disorders and diseases, to learn about the possibility of fitting me with myoelectric arms. This is a type of prosthesis that utilizes the body's neuromuscular system to control the function of an electric-powered hand, wrist, or elbow. But of course there is no feeling or sense of touch.

As I sat with my dad in a large conference room with a team of doctors, one of them was looking at some X-rays of my legs. He asked if I wanted to consider surgery to shorten my left leg—my right leg is three inches shorter than my left—making it easier for me to be fitted for prosthetics.

My arm shot up.

"Excuse me," I said to the doctor. "My dad told me a long time ago that if it works, don't fix it. My legs work fine just the way they are."

That ended all discussion about surgery on my legs. It was also decided that the capabilities of prosthetic hands could not match what I could already do with my existing ones. So that was the last time we ever talked about my getting myoelectric hands.

We left the Shriners hospital thinking they couldn't do anything for me. My mom remembers that first day there, seeing a picture of a young girl, an amputee, doing athletics. She was riding a horse, among other things. Mom thought, *What an inspiration!* About three years later, I was the athlete pictured on another wall and that photo hangs at the hospital to this day, hopefully inspiring even more parents and patients.

Chapter 3

An Uncommon Bond

From the start, my mom understood that strength and support—and not pity—were what I needed. Still, she walked a tenuous line sometimes between treating me like an able-bodied child and feeling a duty to protect me. She scolded me like any other child when I misbehaved.

My mother knew in her heart that for me to have the joys of a normal childhood, I would have to experience things like learning how to ride a bike, or swimming at the public pool. It would be more difficult for me to do these things than other kids, both physically and emotionally, but the reward would be worth far more than the worry and possible injury. "What else could I do?" my mother told me later. "To shield you from everything would have been the worst thing possible."

So she let me try new things, risking bumps, bruises and possible broken bones because she wanted me to be happy. She let me wobble down the street, perched precariously atop a neighbor's bike. Her wisdom trumped her emotion, and as a result I flourished.

I took my first steps at around a year old—in my case, fifteen months. The doctors had said this would not be possible without prosthetics, but contrary to their pronouncements I wobbled across my parents' living room floor in Mountlake Terrace, Washington, a Seattle suburb. Without feet, it was like balancing on stilts.

My dad captured this momentous occasion through the lens of his 8-millimeter camera. My smile, as wide as the Grand Canyon, said it all. He couldn't believe his eyes. My doctors were flabbergasted. From the look on my face, you could see my mind working to physically make the seemingly impossible happen. A friend who watched the home movie commented that we were witnessing "a form of evolution." This was the first of many times that my parents said, "He can do this?"

Children like to imitate other children and I was fortunate to have a brother, Art, who was only twelve months older than I. Art was my "wingman" and you can see him in our home movie, following my fledgling attempts at walking, his arms fully extended toward me in case I fell. He was just as excited as I was at my new skill, giving me a congratulatory hug before I wriggled free to go in a new direction.

Art and I were inseparable. He was also the one who unknowingly helped bring down the protective wall of do's and don'ts. For example, a physical therapist at the hospital had told my mom that she would have to adjust my toys by putting some kind of handles on them. "You need to make adaptations to his surroundings," said the woman, "or Anthony will become frustrated and baffled. You don't want him to feel defeated."

My mother was going to do just that; after all, this woman was an expert in such things. But the day after her appointment she watched me sitting side by side with Art on the living room carpet, surrounded by Legos. While my brother used his hands to build spaceships, castles, and little cars, I used my feet, teeth and "hands" to duplicate my brother's actions.

That's when Mom had an epiphany: I was going to have to adapt to the world; it wasn't going to adapt to me.

This decision altered the course of my life. Rather than becoming "Tony the fragile," I became "Tony the explorer." Rather than becoming the neighborhood boy who can't come out and play, I became the little boy with grass stains on his knees and a skinned elbow who roughhoused just like all the other kids.

My mom knew that when I went to play outside—and then later when I grew up and left home for good—nobody was going to make life easier for me. She wanted to prepare me for that. This was uncharted territory for my parents because they didn't know what I could or could not do. Life was like one continuous experiment, with Art as my leader. I'd watch him do something and then, by trial and error, figure out how I could do the same thing in my own way. What was good for Art was good for me. If Art could play with Legos, so could I. If Art could play cops and robbers, so could I. If Art could ride a bike—a child's greatest symbol of independence and locomotion—I could, too.

Cindy, a neighbor girl who was several years older than Art, was actually the first person to get me on a bike. One day she asked my mom if it would be okay for me to ride her red Schwinn. "I'll help him, I've helped other kids and I'll be really careful," said Cindy.

"Please, Mom!" I said, standing next to Cindy biting my lip and crossing my fingers. Knowing how much I wanted to do this, and how important this was, my mother said, "Sure, go ahead."

Although Mom gave me and Cindy the green light, she couldn't bear to watch so she went inside. I would undoubtedly fall—most kids do—but I had other challenges that other kids did not, like worrying about how to grab the handlebars, losing contact with the pedals, possibly losing concentration because of those things.

Cindy could sense my limitations and was very cautious. "This is all about keeping your balance," she said. "It'll feel a little weird at first, and you might wobble around but just keep pedaling. Pretty soon you will be going straight. Once you get the hang of it, you never forget how to do it."

She held the bike while I hopped on. "Now push off," she said. I now had a crowd of neighborhood kids watching. My brother Art was there, too. To everyone's amazement, I succeeded on the very first attempt. I was a little shaky working my way down the street but I was going under my own power. Cindy had planned to run behind to assist but it was unnecessary. She stopped and watched, slack jawed. "Go Tony! That's awesome!" she squealed as she jumped up and down. The other kids cheered me on and since Mom had left the door open, she could hear what had happened: I had surmounted another barrier.

Of course, this budding new skill was not without its challenges. Without hands, and because my arms are short, my range was limited and I had trouble cornering. At first, all I could do was go straight. Every time I turned, I fell. But after a lot of scrapes, bruises and practice, I was soon weaving in and out of driveways, and up and down our quiet street. I could ride with anybody, including the big boys.

I was thrilled, but I could only ride the bike if Cindy wasn't using it. As luck would have it, Cindy got a new bike a few months later—and a few weeks after that, my parents surprised me on my seventh birthday with the red Schwinn, now outfitted with a banana seat and butterfly handlebars.

Now I was officially one of the neighborhood "gang" that rode bikes in formation up and down the block. I always liked being the leader, and even challenged the other kids to races. When we'd pass my house, I'd shout, "Look Mom, no hands!" It usually put everyone else at ease.

As Art and I grew older my mother gave us a longer "leash." We'd go to the playground at the elementary school a block away.

It was a perfect get-away for kids, complete with a football field and basketball court. We'd sometimes fill our pockets with chalk to draw "parking stalls" for our bikes. The school was far enough away for us to feel independent but close enough to hear Mom call, "Art, Tony. Time to come home!" from the back porch.

When we were in fourth and fifth grades respectively, Art and I would occasionally ride our bikes to the community pool. Although I was not a good swimmer, I loved the water, and enthusiastically jumped into the pool with my brother and friends.

At first I didn't notice that when I got in, some mothers would pull their kids out of the water. Art would say, "Look, everybody else gets out when we get in." It's as though they felt I was contagious, that their kids' hands and feet were going to shrivel up and fall off the minute I touched the water. After a while, I didn't need anybody to point out the exodus to me. Still, I'd just go on swimming, thinking, *Great, more room for us.*

The relationship between Art and me was more one of peers than older brother/younger brother. As much as I wanted to be a normal kid, Art also wanted me to be a normal kid. He didn't automatically do things for me, like pick up my toys, because he knew I could do it myself. But if I ever asked him for help, he was there for me. I rarely did that; I always preferred doing things for myself because it gave me a sense of independence and accomplishment.

My parents treated us equally, including doing all the household chores. I was responsible for picking up, putting away dishes, and general cleaning around the house.

As children, my mom dressed Art and me in the same style of clothes a lot. When we went to the Puyallup Fair, we wore cowboy hats, tan leather coats—she sewed short arms on jackets for me and regular length ones for Art—plaid shirts, and jeans. When we went out to dinner at our favorite pizza place, we'd wear the same button-down collar shirts and similar pants and shoes. Our dark brown hair was also always cut in the same style, with the front combed over to the side that made a big wave. People would stop and ask, "Are they twins?"

Along with being more economical to buy two of everything, I think Mom dressed us alike so people would pay less attention to my not having hands and feet. Instead, they'd see how similar we were; hence, diminishing what appeared unusual about me.

Just because I didn't have hands or feet, that did not mean that I was sickly or delicate. Quite to the contrary, I was the healthiest of all my siblings. My parents never told Art, "Be careful, you might hurt Tony." My behavior never invited that sort of treatment and, like most brothers, wrestling was a primary form of bonding, as well as entertainment. There was no holding back when we tangled; it was all-out war. I'd get him between my legs and squeeze. Unable to escape, Art would squirm and scream, "Let go!" I'd say we were equally matched. I won as many wrestling matches as I lost. Art would disagree. He thinks it was more like 60-40, in his favor.

Art and I had our share of arguments. One time, when we were dueling with our Star Wars light sabers, we ended up in Art's bedroom, which was filled with model cars and paintings.

After a couple of swings, Art said, "Tony, that's enough. You're going to break something."

"Now you're sounding like Mom," I taunted.

With that, I took one last swing with my saber. Art ducked just in the nick of time, and instead of hitting him, I smashed his favorite model car, sending it in several pieces sailing across the room.

Art was furious. "Get out, Tony. Just get out of here."

The fun was over. I told him I was sorry and left the room. But Art didn't hurl insults. There were never any retaliatory attacks, which would have been understandable in a moment of rage.

Never once did he insult me because of my handicap. Anger was no excuse for name calling or cruelty. That's just something Art never did. Besides, it was something my parents would have never tolerated. From the get go, they taught us that we were brothers and needed to respect each other, no matter what might anger us. That went for anyone outside of the family, too: always treat others as you would want to be treated and honor their dignity. We'd get mad at each other, but we were always friends.

Through it all, Art was more than a brother. He was protector, insulator, and, most of all, bosom buddy. But he was also "the other brother." Even as a child, I was the one getting my picture in the local newspaper during a March of Dimes fundraiser, or going on television for a telethon. Relatives would usually want to know how I was doing. Art didn't get the attention.

Being the older brother of someone who always gets the attention quickly loses its luster. He wanted to be recognized and admired too. As early as I can remember, he was always doing art work. My gift was social. Most of the time, I was outgoing. I loved people. They endlessly fascinated me. Art was more interested in the solitary act of creating things to look at. Wanting to excel at something he could consider his own, Art drew paintings and made models of cars, ships, and planes. His room became an ever-changing art exhibit. It was something that didn't interest me, and gave him his own identity separate from "Tony's brother."

While I never cried about not having hands and feet, once when I was about five years old, I asked my mom matter-of-factly, "Will I ever have hands like Art?"

She hesitated for a moment and then said, "You'll get hands when you're the same age as your brother."

Naturally, I would never be the same age as Art. My mom wasn't sure I understood that twist, but the answer seemed to suffice. I didn't ask about growing hands ever again.

I was never pitied by either family or friends. It wasn't allowed or expected. In fact, because of my go-get-'em approach to life, it never crossed their minds. "I don't ever remember Tony feeling sorry for himself," my mom would tell her friends. "He never blamed God or asked 'why me?' He's always accepted who he is and it never held him back."

People who knew me could never feel sorry for me. It was only the people who didn't know me—the strangers at the mall or in a restaurant, the people who saw me only an arm's length away or more—who pitied.

I was fortunate to have such a loving family and a storybook-like friendship with Art. And it was a birth defect that brought us so close together.

I always wanted to mimic Art and he tried his best to make sure I could keep up, even if it meant he had to slow down a little. He showed tremendous patience with me, something I saw in my own son when he was an infant, when I would for example tie his shoes.

So many times my brother has said, "What amazes me about Tony is that he has made an opportunity out of a hardship. If I had been born without hands or feet, I could never have done what he's done. Tony is remarkable. He is truly blessed."

Yet the triumph wasn't mine alone. My accomplishments weren't solo flights. Art was the co-pilot, the navigator, and quite simply, the wind beneath my wings.

Chapter 4

Familiar Faces

The days were getting gradually shorter. Summer was winding down and I would be starting my first day of school today at St. Pius X, a small Catholic school that teaches respect for authority and for each other, while setting high academic standards. I was a little nervous, mainly because I wouldn't know anyone and I was excited to be meeting new friends. Art would be in the classroom next to me so I would see him a lot, but would have the chance to branch out on my own.

Sister Barbara Rabane, B.V.M., a tall and slender woman with short, brownish hair, introduced herself to us as our new first-grade teacher. Mom said she was the perfect person for a child to transition from mother to teacher. She had a calm, direct demeanor but was very loving. My parents had already prepared her for my arrival, so she acted the same to me as she did to the other children.

I did get some curious stares from my new classmates, but no one said anything to me. A few weeks after the start of school, the students asked Sister Rabane, "Why doesn't he have hands and feet?"

"That's the way God made him," she responded. "That was God's plan for him."

Sister Rabane knew that the other children should understand more about my disability. The more educated they were about me, the less my condition would be an "issue" for them. Indeed, it would help them comprehend and respect all people with handicaps.

"Boys and girls, please go to the back of the room and sit on the green carpet," she instructed. "As we all know, Anthony has artificial feet, called prosthetics, to help him walk. Many of you have been asking questions about this, so I would like him to show you how they work. Anthony, could you please remove them and explain how they work to the class?"

"Yes, Sister," I responded. Uninhibited, I took off my "feet" and walked around the green carpet on my stumps, smiling as I went around in a circle in front of them proudly answering their questions. I was not self-conscious about being different. Then I took my prostheses and passed them around the room. The Sister didn't ask me to do this, I just liked to share. The kids held them and then touched my stumps.

Everyone was somewhat in awe. This was the perfect icebreaker and helped the other children become comfortable with my condition. We became a tight-knit group after this, and I loved going to school.

I guess I became a walking, talking lesson, something that can't be taught in a textbook. Sister Rabane later told me that I became an agent of perception, helping my classmates—as well as teachers—dissolve bigotry and stereotypes.

While I didn't know about these things at my age, I was aware of the view that if you're missing an arm or a leg, or had some kind of disability, less was expected of you. I rebelled against that even as a first grader—championing what would become a lifelong mission.

Like any first grader, I had to learn to print. Without hands, Sister Rabane worried if I would be able to keep up with the penmanship drills. But I surprised her. My handwriting became exceptional. I'd clamp the pencil between the two bones of my right arm and write perfectly executed letters. Soon, she was holding up my assignment for the classroom to see. "Can anyone else print as well as this?"

My fourth-grade teacher was Sister Isadora Lorentz, B.V.M., an ex-Chicago police officer turned nun who possessed a grandmotherly quality. She said that she saw me as someone who wanted to show the world what I could do.

I did this in the classroom and in the cerebral world of books. I always wanted to be the best version of me that I could, and St. Pius X nurtured this desire for academic excellence. For at least an hour every night in grade school I would sit with my mom at the kitchen table with my head buried in my books. Sometimes she'd be reading a magazine, waiting for the inevitable question, "Is this right?" Usually she responded with a nod or "That looks good to me." It took several years of such reassurances until I had the confidence to do my homework on my own (which I sometimes did hanging upside down from the couch). With the helpful prodding of a diligent mother and caring teachers, I got A's and B's in all my years at St. Pius X.

I also proved to others that my disability couldn't hold me back in the world of recess and gym class—a surprise to many. "He has no feet, so how can he run so fast?" Sister Rabane would ask the other teachers as they stood outside and watched. Although my teachers worried, I insisted in being included in all outdoor activities. From soccer to basketball to football to kickball, I participated in everything all the other children did. I was given free reign, anything less and I would have considered myself "different" or an "outsider." What could be better than kicking a soccer ball to a friend who scores a goal, or catching a pass from your best pal?

While kickball was one of my favorite sports, it had a built-in risk. The act of kicking occasionally resulted in my prosthesis flying across the playground, landing with a thud next to a startled classmate. For me, it was no big deal. I'd quickly retrieve my leg, or someone would fetch it for me. With a couple of tugs and shoves, the prosthesis was back on and I was up and running again, chasing down the ball.

In second grade, I decided to ride my red Schwinn to school. During recess, I was reluctantly given approval to ride it once around the playground. As I pumped the pedals of my bike, circling the borders of the fenced-in playground, my classmates watched and cheered. I turned and waved. The nuns breathed a collective sigh of relief.

As I continued to prove myself, my teachers quickly overcame their concerns about my falling and getting hurt. They soon learned I could handle myself just like anybody else. As far as they were concerned, I *was* like anyone else. I'd become Tony, just another student; not Tony, the special-needs student. And the last thing I wanted was special treatment.

They later told me they still felt a sense of wonder as they watched this little disfigured boy go through each day with an "isn't-life-grand" smile. My motto was "If you show me, I can do it."

If there was something I couldn't do, like use scissors, one of the other students would help me. Arnel Ramac, a classmate from first to eighth grade, became my second pair of hands. All I needed to do was get my lunch pail out, and he would quietly get up and punch the straw through my juice carton and then return to his seat. Nothing was said. It was a little thing, but it was an example of the bond that existed between me and my classmates. I would never have asked Arnel for help because I was so stubborn—he just did it.

Early on, I became a minor class celebrity because I was a good storyteller, and I loved making my classmates laugh. I was good at telling jokes, and I liked playing innocent tricks. Of course, I'd tell them about my being on the occasional telethon over the weekend or about having my picture in the local weekly newspaper during a fundraiser for The March of Dimes.

As a result, I never really had reason to defend myself. St. Pius X also had strict rules even back then about bullying and fighting. Violators faced suspension from school, pending the verdict of a jury of parents and teachers in the principal's office.

Once as a sixth grader, I did come close to throwing and taking a couple of blows. A misunderstanding with Shawn, a classmate, ended up with us squaring off in the playground during a recess.

Shawn said, "I don't care if you are handicapped."

There was dead silence. As soon as he blurted out those angry words, Shawn immediately apologized. I told him to forget about it. He begged me not to tell the nuns.

"Don't worry about it," I told him. And my biggest feud of grade school was over.

When I was a fourth grader, Sister Isadora, who trained the altar boys, asked me, "Aren't you going to be an altar boy?"

This innocent question would eventually change the course of my life. I hesitated. "I can't." It was the only time Sister Isadora heard me say I couldn't do something.

"Why not?" she asked with a puzzled look. I didn't respond. It seemed too complicated. "I think it's something you can do," she said softly.

So I accepted the challenge. I learned how to handle the sacraments, when to light the candles and where to stand and kneel during Mass. The only thing I struggled with was pouring from the curate because my arms were so short. To compensate, the priest, Father Armstrong, S.J., simply lowered his arms as I poured the water for him to wash his hands. Art was also an altar boy and Father Armstrong paired us up at the suggestion of my mother, just in case. But I never spilled, never knocked over a candle, never fell asleep during a service, and certainly never showed up late in the four years I worked as an altar boy. I enjoyed Mass and never thought about how many people were there that day or if people were watching me.

It was during Mass that Jane Edwards, the wife of a doctor from Edmonds, Cam Stewart, first noticed me. Because she knew that the Shriners helped kids with disabilities, she wanted to see if there was anything else that could be done for me. Jane wasn't really familiar with us and not comfortable discussing this directly with my parents so she went to Sister Isadora to offer her help. Sister Isadora then phoned my parents. This kindness eventually led to my going to the Shriners Hospital for Children in Portland, Oregon, when I was fourteen. This is a world-class facility that delivers the highest quality of care to children with various orthopedic and neuromusculoskeletal disorders and diseases. They fitted me with the proper prosthetics.

I am so grateful to Sister Rabane and Sister Isadora, who helped me understand that things happen for a reason and not by accident, and that God had a plan for my life. That's part of my strength today. That's what inspires me.

Sister Rabane had told me there was a presence about me that she couldn't put her finger on, that you "can't analyze."

My "I'll-overcome-anything" attitude had a lasting effect upon my classmates and my teachers. They didn't forget the little boy who had four good reasons for being bitter, reclusive, and despondent. Instead, I was blessed with the inner resourcefulness to do well in the classroom and to make friends. Maybe it was God-given, maybe it was the way my parents nurtured me, or maybe it was a combination of both. Whatever it was, it led to my belief that people—with or without handicaps—can make the most of their situations through a positive outlook, a willingness to try anything, and the belief that quitting is not an option.

Sister Isadora said one of her life's greatest privileges was to have me as a student. It amazed and humbled me to hear her say that. Occasionally, my teachers used me as a model for how to overcome hardships and challenges. Sister Isadora said, "I'd use you, Tony, as an example for the students who were feeling sorry for themselves. I'd ask them, 'What would you do if you were walking around without hands or feet?' That put their problems in a different light."

I was not without role models of my own. When I was ten, one of my favorite TV shows was *The Incredible Hulk*, starring Bill Bixby as a brilliant but undersized scientist, and a bodybuilder named Lou Ferrigno as his enormous green alter ego. My fascination with Lou went beyond his size and color. Although I respected him for his athletic accomplishments, I respected him even more for overcoming his hearing deficit.

In 1982 I asked my parents to buy me his book, *The Incredible Lou Ferrigno*. I read about how he was teased and picked on as a child due to his hearing loss. I read how he used that teasing as a source of motivation to ultimately become, as his book title describes, incredible! He wanted to be so big and strong that nobody else would ever dare tease him again.

One Saturday morning my dad came into my room and told me to get dressed—and to grab my new book. We loaded up in the car and off we went—to the Safeway store. Safeway? Why on earth would my dad tell me to bring my new book for a trip to the grocery store?

When we pulled into the lot I noticed an unusually large number of cars parked outside, and as we got out of the car, I noticed other people walking into the store holding a copy of *The Incredible*

Lou Ferrigno. Inside the store a frenzied crowd swarmed around a table near the front. As we got closer my dad picked me up so I could see over the mob. As I looked past what seemed like a mile of people my eyes finally found the center of the commotion: there sat the Incredible Hulk himself, Lou Ferrigno!

Lou was furiously signing book after book after book. As my dad put me back down he said, "Tony, you need to push your way to the front if you want your book signed." I nodded and turned toward the crowd with one single purpose: to work my way through it.

Pushing and weaving, I fought through the mass of bodies for what seemed like forever, but finally made it to the front of the line and stood squarely in front of the signing table. Lou's head was down as he signed another person's book. He finished and said "Next . . . " without looking up.

I placed my book on the table and started to push it toward him. As he reached out for it he saw my hand and raised his head to look me in the eye. Then he pushed his chair back from the table and rose to his feet. The crowd went silent as he came to his full height of 6'5": the Incredible Lou Ferrigno! With the table between us he reached down, put his giant hands around my chest and lifted me into his arms. I felt like I was ascending to the heavens. He set me down next to him and asked my name. Then he took my book, opened it and wrote, "To Tony, Always Stay Tough—Lou Ferrigno."

Twelve years later I was invited to Chicago to receive a special achievement award from the National Italian American Sports Hall of Fame. (Why was I invited to an "Italian American" event, you ask? I had been asked to this affair because of my Italian heritage. As for my last name, which does not sound Italian, my grandfather intentionally dropped the "a", as was common for immigrants at the time. Thus "Volpentesta" became "Volpentest.") To my surprise and delight, one of the athletes to be inducted into the Hall of Fame at the event was Lou Ferrigno!

When I arrived at the hotel I noticed a commotion at the check-in desk: Lou towering over a petite hotel hostess and arguing about a mix-up with his room. I walked up and tapped him on the shoulder. He turned to see who would dare interrupt him while he was engaged in a heated conversation. When he saw me his shoulders relaxed and he smiled. "I met you when you were a little boy," he said.

I was shocked; he actually remembered me.

At the dinner the next evening I gave a speech and watched, somewhat star-struck, as various athletes received their awards. I wanted to ask Lou for another autograph but the timing was never right.

Then, the next morning, I woke up top find that a couple pieces of paper had been slid under my door. One was a photograph of Lou signed, "To Tony, You're a true role model and a wonderful human being—Your Friend Lou Ferrigno." The other was a letter: "Hi Tony, I was really moved by your words last night. Don't forget that evening and know that people love you and like I said to you, this is the beginning for you. You can reach the moon now in whatever you decide to do. I'm proud to be a part of your life! From L.F."

The words inspired me, and almost immediately I had an opportunity to pass their meaning on. A friend of my parents called and told me about Curt Busch, a third grader at St. Pius X, who was supposed to bring pictures of his family to display in his classroom for show-and-tell. But he said to his mother, LeAnn, "I want to bring Tony."

"What about your family pictures?" she asked.

"That's okay," Curt answered. "We'll just put Tony's pictures up."

His mother was surprised by Curt's infatuation with me. I guess I became the first substitute for family photos in the history of the school. I accepted the invitation and returned to the school I grew up in, and spoke to the class.

Six of my eight teachers at St. Pius X were nuns. I was taught by amazing women, who were committed to teaching, to their church and to God. For them, education was a calling, not a profession. I was so grateful to have them and I gave school my all.

My years at St. Pius X were special and helped me believe in myself and realize that all things really were possible.

Chapter 5

A Small Fish in a Big Pond

My years at St. Pius X were happy and comforting. Come September every year, I'd look forward to seeing the familiar faces of my friends and classmates, just as I had the year before and the year before that.

There was no need for introductions or explanations that I was born without hands and feet. I knew everyone by name. Maybe only one or two new students joined my class each school year—sometimes none at all. St. Pius X was my safe haven, my home away from home. Though I might encounter insensitive people making callous remarks or engaging in not-so-subtle stares out in the general public, nothing of the sort ever happened at school. The nuns had a zero-tolerance policy for name-calling and insisted that we respect and have empathy for one another. It was an ideal setting for someone like me, who could have been an easy target for ridicule.

But the years passed all too quickly and before I knew it I was a ninth-grader, and in high school. It felt so very foreign to me—a radical change of scenery as though I had been dropped onto a different planet. Instead of seeing the same thirty friendly faces each day in my grade school, it was thirty different faces in each classroom at Woodway High School. St. Pius X had 250 students total, while Woodway had 1,400.

Going from parochial school to a large public school was also a big shock. We were pretty sheltered at St. Pius X because everything was so structured. This high school environment was far less so. Rather than a fairly homogenous group of kids, there were all different types of students. A really big thing for me was not having a dress code. We never had to worry about what to wear to school with the St. Pius X uniform—and that rule brought with it a sense of cohesion. A lot of wealthy families sent their kids to Woodway so there was a vast difference in the way they dressed compared with the general population of students. Suddenly what you wore became a status symbol—though I was never really much concerned about that.

Thus the transition from St. Pius X to high school was particularly painful and drawn out. At St. Pius X I had everything figured out, it was all routine. By eighth grade I was on top of the heap; now I was a small fish in a big pond, with a disability to boot. Adolescents just want to blend in and be one of the crowd; I certainly could not do that!

There was not much time between classes and even when I did have time, I didn't stop to socialize or hang out at my locker, which I actually did not use freshman year. It was physically difficult because I had to balance the books and folders between my waist and the locker to free up both "hands" to be able to manipulate the lock. Rather than do this, it just seemed easier to carry all of my supplies and books in my backpack. Once I was more comfortable (after freshman year) I started to use the locker. But that first year, between classes I just rushed through the hallways.

Although I had always been an outgoing person, in this new environment I grew very wary and timid. The more people stared at me, the more isolated and lonely I felt. It could be they weren't staring at or talking about me at all, but after a while I became a prisoner of my own mind. School wasn't enjoyable anymore. This transition year was a difficult time in my life and the days seemed interminable.

I felt particularly uncomfortable in the unregulated social atmosphere of the cafeteria, where you could easily pick out which kids were in each social group. There were the intellectual "nerds" in one corner; the rebellious punkers dressed all in black in another; the jocks and their perky cheerleader girlfriends in another. I was just one of the "regular Joes" which was really a catch-all for all the people who were not in a group.

Some of the teachers said they would be available for questions or extra help at lunchtime. I started doing this and noticed that a few of the kids just stayed and ate their lunches in there. The teachers didn't mind so I took to eating in a classroom, sometimes alone, sometimes with a handful of other students, for all of my freshman year. This was my sanctuary. I really didn't mind, I could eat in peace and not have to worry about the whispers and the stares.

I suppose it wasn't all bad. I had a few friends from St. Pius X at the new school and, as the year wore on, I got more comfortable and was able to loosen up, make a few friends and have fun.

I lasted through freshman year and by the time I was a sophomore things were a little easier for me. Kids weren't so shocked by my appearance anymore and the school was at least familiar to me now.

A chance incident in P.E. one day set me on a course that would change my life forever. "Okay, today we are going to play touch football," said the teacher. Instead of dividing the teams, he would pick two captains to choose their own teammates. I settled in for the long wait. I was pretty much always picked last for all these team sports. Who could blame the captains for thinking that? How could someone without hands or feet possibly play football?

Once the teams were picked we were out on the field. I wondered what I would do. I actually already knew that I was a great receiver from the many times I would play catch in the street with my brothers Mike and Art. I actually could throw quite well too. My modified shoes weren't the greatest for running but I was pretty decent anyways. The other team, however, saw me as no threat at all so they didn't even cover me when I went out for a pass. I was always way downfield, wide open in the end zone, but our quarterback never threw me the ball.

On one of those plays, Joe Hampson, one of the "jocks" who was on the sidelines for this play spotted me alone at the five-yard line and yelled to our quarterback, "Throw it to Tony! Throw it to Tony!"

Did I hear that right? I thought. Joe was one of the popular crowd of kids. He was tall, good-looking, and though I didn't really know him all that well, he was always friendly and nice to me. Still, it surprised me that he would do this.

The quarterback scrambled from the defenders, apparently hesitant to squander the down on me.

"Throw it to him!" Joe called.

To my shock, the quarterback let loose with a bomb. The ball wobbled through the blue sky and came down with a thud into my arms. Finally, somebody had thrown me the ball! I clamped onto to it, clutching it as if I were hugging the golden goose and scrambled for the goal line. The kid with no hands and feet had just scored a touchdown.

I celebrated with the rest of my teammates. I knew I was more than capable of catching the pass, I was just surprised that the quarterback actually threw it to me. The opposing team never left me open again.

The next time we played football the teacher again picked two captains: Joe and Bill. I braced for the certainty of being picked last, as usual. Bill picked first. "Sam," he said, raising both fists in the air. Sam was big and burly and could catch the ball one-handed. I leaned against the wall, prepared for the long wait. Joe raised his chin, his eyes scanning the crowd. "Tony!" he called.

Huh? Did I hear right? Is there another Tony here? I thought to myself. I was as shocked. I hesitated.

"Yeah, you, Tony. Come on down!" said Joe cheerfully. "After what you did last time, you're a game changer!" Talk about a great feeling!

After that, I didn't feel excluded anymore.

At the end of the game I floated to the locker room. "Hey Tony," said Joe. "I've noticed the reason you always get downfield is because you've got a lot of speed. You should come out for the track team with me. Tryouts are coming up soon."

"What, you mean; like to be the manager?" I asked. He certainly couldn't mean I'd be one of the actual athletes.

Joe laughed. "No, as a runner! Why would you try out to be a manager?"

"I'll let you in on a secret: I don't have any feet," I quipped. I felt comfortable enough with Joe to resurrect my happy, self-deprecating personality.

"Yeah, I did see that," he said. "And I also saw how fast you can run with those little shoes. What have you got to lose?" he asked. "Think about it. You have a little time."

"Okay, I'll think about it," I told him.

At that time, I was wearing half shoes, designed by an orthopedist on the Shriners Hospital staff. It was like a shoe with no toes, with extra material wrapped around so that the front of the shoe curved up. They simply slipped over my stumps. Could I actually try out for the track team wearing these things?

Later that night, I talked with my brother, Art, and told him what happened. Art had little interest in sports, organized or otherwise. I had played on the elementary school basketball team, but hadn't done anything else that was organized. But high school track? That was a whole different animal.

"I can tell that you really want to do this—you just don't believe you can," Art told me. "You would get on the team no matter what."

"Huh?" I said, surprised.

"Yeah, they take everyone. If you do the workouts, you're on the team. You get points for how well you do in the meets, and if you accumulate enough points during the season, while competing on the varsity team, you would earn a letter in track."

"Oh," I said, still thinking.

"You know I'm more of a 'mathlete' than an athlete," said Art. "But I will make you a deal: if you go, I will, too."

"You're on!" I said.

I was still a little sheepish about this, even with Art by my side. Even with a "no cut" policy, would they even let me try out?

One day, there was open gym after school so I went in to play basketball. I was "in the zone" that day, and I seemed to be hitting everything I threw up in the air—even from "way downtown" it was nothing but net. Mr. Anderson, who was also the boys' track coach, was reorganizing the storage area and was in and out of the gym. Feeling particularly confident, I decided to approach him.

"Mr. Anderson, you're the head track coach aren't you?" I asked.

"Why, yes I am," he replied.

"My name is Tony Volpentest and I was thinking about trying out for the team and wanted to get your thoughts on that."

"I don't see a problem with it. If I may ask," he replied. "Will you need any special treatment? I've got a lot of kids I am responsible for."

"No. I only want to run," I told him. "Treat me like all the other kids. No special treatment for me."

He smiled and shook his head in agreement, "Good, Tony, because I wasn't going to give you any!"

Chapter 6

All Guts, No Glory

The first day of tryouts finally rolled around. Some kids would show up and run just to see if they had the skills needed to compete, while others would come out and try various events to see if they even liked them. I didn't expect to do well, unless they included a running-on-heels event. What really motivated me, deep down, was to make friends, become involved and be part of a team. I remembered how much I liked being part of a group at St. Pius X. The day I scored that touchdown in the P.E. football game gave me a whole new perspective. Kids treated me differently after that catch—and it felt good.

I looked around at the crowd. I was glad Art was there with me. We made small talk as we waited. There must have been about eighty boys. After the introductions Coach Anderson divided us into groups, then it was time to start. "Boys, listen up," he said. "The first event is the 100." He then ran a couple of heats until he got to my group.

I was pretty nervous as I went to the starting line and took a couple of deep breaths. I looked down at everyone's feet. They all had regular looking running shoes in all different sizes and colors, but they all looked pretty much the same. My odd-looking half-shoes definitely did not look like the others.

Coach blew the whistle signaling us to start. I ran without any other prosthetics. Since my left leg was three inches longer than my right, my running motion was a labored rocking back and forth. Smooth? Not exactly! If anyone had a good excuse for quitting track, it would have been me. I had to work twice as hard to get half as far as everyone else and over time my stumps developed sores from my awkward running style.

Is this what I have to endure to make friends? I thought. But to me, it was worth it.

The workouts were grueling, and were held five days a week for one to two hours. Lots of kids quit, quickly finding out that track was no pleasure cruise. I went religiously and participated like everyone else. In fact, in three years on the track team, I never missed a single practice. Only once did I ask to forego a drill.

"Today we're going to work on the 4x100-relay," said Coach Anderson. "The teams that win aren't just the teams with the fastest runners—they are the teams that master the baton pass."

I gulped. How the heck was I going to do this? The coach was assigning runners to groups spaced about 30 yards apart around the track. He trotted across the field in his blue jogging sweats, shouting orders.

"Coach, do I have to do this?" I asked. "Of course you do! I want everyone doing this," he snapped.

Naturally, I struggled with the drill. I dropped the baton on my first exchange, but I stuck with it. Persistence paid off and eventually I got the hang of it. In fact, by my senior year, I was leading the varsity's best relay squad and my exchanges were flawless. I never muffed a single handoff in a meet as a senior.

Discussing this surprising skill in an interview years later, Coach Anderson said, "That was all him. How do you show a kid without hands how to pass a baton? I had no idea. I didn't know what to do. I showed him the basics, but it was up to him to figure out how to do it. He never backed down from anything. That's the most amazing thing about Tony. He never backed down from anything!"

In the relay, timing is everything: If you are receiving the baton you must accurately gauge how fast the incoming runner is approaching and time your take-off appropriately. If you're giving the baton you must also estimate your speed and call out to your teammate when you "hit their mark" to let them know when to take off. As the lead-off runner in high school I always started on the corner and ran the curve making sure to stay tight to the inside of the lane. The person I would hand off to would position himself on the outside of the lane so there could be a tiny bit of overlap while the actual exchange took place. The fact that my arms are shorter made this step even more important to make sure our legs wouldn't get tangled up.

Of course running is the meat and potatoes of track, but the basic body mechanics of it offered major challenges for me. Because I had no toes—which act as a runner's launching pad—my quadriceps had to work overtime. This gave me little more than an up-and-down piston motion, like running on your heels. My hamstrings and calf muscles were merely going along for the ride. All I could do was pick up and put down my "feet," robbing me of the most important aspect in running—pulling with the hamstrings and pushing with the quads. With only a portion of my legs doing the work, I fatigued fast as my quadriceps quickly give out.

Sometimes, at the end of a series of 300-meter sprints, my legs felt like cement blocks. Unable to hold myself up, I would stumble and fall down in exhaustion. The first time this happened, I collapsed on the track. Coach Anderson kept his word, however. He gave me no special favors. Crumpled in a heap on the gravel, gasping for air, I heard Coach's booming voice, reminding me of our deal. "Tony," he barked. "If you're going to fall, fall onto the grass. Don't fall onto the track."

With runners sprinting by, I rolled over onto the field and stayed there until I could catch my breath. In his defense, Mr. Anderson's reprimand was far more than just "tough love:" his biggest fear was that other runners could trample me. The safest place to recuperate was on the grass.

My sophomore year, I ran on the junior varsity team and finished last in every race. Not surprisingly, I did not beat a single able-bodied runner. I usually finished the race as much as 30 meters behind the second-to-last runner, a considerable margin in a 200-meter race. I'd lose by five or six seconds. While this doesn't sound like much, in a short race like the 200 where the high school finishing times are in the 23 to 24-second range, it's a huge gap. For a lot of kids, getting these kinds of results—after hour upon hour of side aches, sweating and grueling workouts—would be enough reason to quit. I never gave it a second thought. I was achieving my initial goal of making friends. I was slowly becoming one of the boys.

I always gave it my all on each and every drill. I never heard Coach Anderson's booming prod, "Let's pick it up, Volpentest" because my effort was never in question. My performance, however, was a different matter.

During my sophomore year, my times in the 100 meters did drop—from 16.9 to 14.3 seconds—and I knocked several seconds off my 200-meter time of 31 seconds. But considering I was bobbling around the track on toeless stumps with shoes not designed for athletics, my commitment to training for a perennial last place spot was inspiring to many. I also won the "Most Inspirational" award at the end of the track year.

I had achieved my goal of making some friends, and now I wanted to improve, to better my times. Making friends got me here, but a competitive desire is what kept me here. It would be a tall order; sometimes, I was barely halfway through a race when the winner was crossing the finish line. But that didn't really faze me. I enjoyed running. I liked pushing myself and seeing what I could do. Could I knock a second or two off my best time? Why not? It became an all-consuming challenge, not that anyone else would care. My times wouldn't be posted in school logs for people to admire years after I had graduated. I was not running against any opponents, only my own limitations. I was running in a one-man race, and was getting better, little by little. They were tiny improvements but to me, they were a huge deal.

Chapter 7

Real-Life Blade Runner

During the spring of my sophomore year, I chanced upon something intriguing—track competitions for kids with missing limbs. They featured it on a television special I just happened to watch. I was dumbfounded as well as curious. How well would I do against someone with disabilities like mine? I had a funny feeling I wouldn't be finishing last.

For some reason I mentioned it to Ms. Hall, my German class teacher. A kind, but very direct woman with a no-nonsense demeanor, she intimidated some students. However, I was always comfortable around her. Maybe it was because she reminded me of my father in the sense that she was very strict and I liked the structure. I always felt that she took a genuine interest in me, wanting to make sure I was doing alright.

I discovered there was an upcoming event in Tampa, Florida. When I told Ms. Hall about the meet, and upon seeing how passionate I was about it, she made it her mission to see that I could go. "Tell me, Tony, how serious are you about running?" she asked.

"When I run, I'm free of judgments and inhibitions," I told her. "I want to see how far I can go. But I don't think my family can afford my going to Tampa." Just getting there would be expensive, let alone the lodging, the meals and the event fees. Not to mention the logistics: The distance from Seattle to Tampa was nearly 4,000 miles.

"This would be a great experience for you," she said. "Let's find a way to raise the money you need. I'll ask friends and foes, acquaintances and strangers. The worst that can happen is they say no."

Susan Hall literally went door to door, business to business—to grocery stores, banks, health clubs, friends, and neighbors. She even got donations from the Nordstrom family, owners of the upscale department store chain. Single-handedly, she raised a whopping $2,000. It covered my expenses and even allowed for my father to travel with me.

It would be a trip that would change my life.

I got to Tampa, and finally it was time to race. While racing was not new to me, competition in this context was. A lot of people had worked to get me here; could I meet their expectations as well as my own?

I was in the starting blocks for the 100-meter race. I was more nervous than usual, maybe because so many people had worked so hard to get me all the way here. I looked right, and then left, shaking my arms to loosen them up, rolling my head and shrugging my shoulders. I breathed in, and then out, trying to relax.

Looking to my left, there was the famous Dennis Oehler—the Hollywood handsome superstar. A triple gold-medal winner at the Seoul Paralympics the previous year, and a world record holder. He was famous, and well thought of, and had brought a great deal of credibility to this sport. He was also one of the first disabled athletes to make a living from product endorsements and appearance fees. To my amazement, although fourteen years my senior, he was allowed to compete in the junior division as an exhibition.

Oehler calmly settled his body into the starting blocks. On his right leg he wore a black, high-tech prosthetic device; I wore my usual half shoes.

The starter fired his gun and we were off. Not surprisingly, Oehler crossed the finish line long before I did. In fact, although I came in first amongst the competitors in my division, I was so far behind Oehler that I felt as if this were just another high school track meet.

Oehler turned and walked back slowly toward the rest of the field of runners. His hand shot out to greet me as I plodded across the finish line in second place. He greeted us all and congratulated us. He was so fast, I was in awe.

Fortunately for me, since his involvement was just an exhibition, his time didn't count. He was participating as a crowd pleaser. And he was just that. The crowd roared. To say his story was inspirational is an understatement.

In April 1984, Oehler, a former high-school soccer star who had just signed a contract with a professional team, was a passenger in a friend's car. It was a slick, rainy night and they were driving down the Long Island Expressway in New York when the car stalled. Oehler jumped out to push it off the road when not one, but two cars hit him. Miraculously, he lived, and the next thing he knew, he was in a hospital recovery room. His right foot had been crushed and doctors told him that they had no choice but to amputate his leg about nine inches below the knee. His promising soccer career was over.

Not untypically, his girlfriend of twelve years walked out on him. She just assumed he wouldn't be able to care for himself and she didn't want that responsibility. Oehler grew despondent, believing he would be on crutches or in a wheelchair for the rest of his life. He turned to alcohol for solace and considered suicide.

However later that summer a friend drove him to the International Games for the Disabled in Valley Stream, not far from where Oehler lived. He was astonished by what he saw. Other amputees like him were flying down the track. He asked one of the track officials what was the world record for amputees in the 100-meter dash. At the time, it was 12.8 seconds.

Five years later, at the 1988 Paralympic Games in Seoul, South Korea, Oehler took possession of the new world record with a time of 11.73, shaving off more than a second from the previous one.

With this in mind, losing a race to Dennis Oehler was nothing to be ashamed of. I needed to put my "loss" into perspective. Still, I couldn't help feeling disappointed—and on that day I determined to never again lose a race in an amputee event.

Still, I ended up doing pretty well in Tampa. At that meet, I ran the 60-, 100- and 200-meter races, finishing with times of 8.95 seconds, 14.38 seconds and 31.08 seconds respectively. When I first entered, I figured I'd finish in the middle of the pack because many of these athletes had for years been racing competitively in this kind of venue. To my surprise, I sprinted my way to three gold medals!

Ironically, Oehler gave me some unintentional help that day. Prior to the race I had had the opportunity to listen to him give a speech in which he described his world-record runs from Seoul in 1988—including how right before the race he could close his eyes and feel the sun hitting his skin, and the sweat running down his cheek.

From this description I learned a lot about visualization—a tool I would use in every subsequent race I ran.

Yet when I visualized that first race, what I saw was not my stance or my form; what I saw was Dennis Oehler reaching out to greet me as I hobbled over the finish line in distant second place. His had been such a confident gesture—so smooth, so self-assured. A gentlemen's gesture that nevertheless said, "It couldn't really have ended any other way, now could it?" I knew right then and there that one day, I'd be walking back to the finish line to greet him.

That became my focus, my obsession, the fire to temper my athletic skills.

Winning three gold medals was a thrill beyond words. I had managed to justify the faith of those who had helped pay my way. I was ecstatic. But other good things happened to me at this event as well.

After I won my second gold medal, a stranger came up and introduced himself as Van Phillips. He told me that in 1977 he had lost his leg below the knee in a water-skiing accident. After wallowing for a while in depression, he turned something negative into something incredibly positive: he designed and developed a lightweight carbon graphite prosthetic foot for himself. It proved so effective that he launched a company, based in California, called Flex-Foot. He, of course, was wearing his product and demonstrated it for me. I recognized it as the twin of the device Oehler had worn in our race.

"I see some real potential with you, and I think the Flex-Foot could really help propel you into that next level," Phillips told me. "In fact, I believe in you—and the feet—so much that I'd like to provide you with two feet and pay for you to travel to New York later this summer."

I instantly accepted.

Ms. Hall once again went to work on my behalf. She phoned Mark Schone, a physical therapist who had worked on her back following surgery. She wanted to help me get stronger, but she didn't know any personal trainers. Mark was the closest thing to a personal trainer. She told him that there wasn't enough money to pay him, but asked if he would be willing to help me prepare for my next race.

Mark agreed. He had some advanced equipment, which although was primarily used for PT, worked very well to strengthen my legs. He also worked with me on other equipment as the facility was also a full gym. For the next two months, I worked under Schone's expert supervision.

Four weeks after Tampa, my two Flex-Feet—attached to brand new prostheses—and I competed in the junior division of a national amputee competition in New York City. I ended up running 14.30 in the 100 meters and 30.50 in the 200 meters, both of which were first place finishes in the junior division.

The new "feet" were revolutionary and an absolute blessing. When I worked out on the track I wore these "blades," black J-shaped carbon-graphite prosthetic feet seven inches tall. My track shoes were secured to the base of these blades, and the upper ends were attached to sturdy prosthetic sockets, which slipped over my real legs and were tightly strapped on.

Finally, I was running on the front two inches of my "feet." It is as if I had toes for the very first time. Hence, I now had the energy return of real feet. Until then, I had been running on stumps, bobbing down the track. Now I was the author of a proper and more normal running style. Still, I had to learn how to run—the right way—all over again.

As much as the blades improved the mechanics of running, there were other challenges. The manufacturer had supplied me with "feet" in many degrees of stiffness. And both of my legs are not the same length. My right leg is three inches shorter than my left. One degree of stiffness might be just right for my right leg, but not for my left. If a "foot" is too stiff, it doesn't provide enough spring. If it's too soft, it doesn't generate enough energy return, causing me to be out of sync.

The permutations seemed infinite and something that felt okay on one day could feel completely different on the next. It was frustrating at first but after lots of trial and error and seemingly endless swapping out we settled on the proper ones for me to use.

Oehler was not participating in the national amputee competition in New York City, but he was there. I hung two photos of him—cut out of a magazine—on the wall of the dorm room I was staying in at Hofstra University. One showed Oehler in midstride in front of a blurry background, creating the illusion of rapid speed. The other photo was of him working out with Carl Lewis—the sprinter and long jumper—who had won nine Olympic gold medals.

Those photos became my fixation. I studied them. I wanted to be the one in the ad. I wanted to be the one that other runners pointed to and whispered to each other, "There he is."

At one time there had been no reason to believe I could beat Oehler, let alone replace him as the famous face in the magazines. Now there was no excuse. We were both wearing Flex-Feet. And yet my 100-meter time was nearly three seconds slower than Oehler's. That's like getting lapped in a 1,600-meter race. To beat Oehler, even to *think* I could beat him, was wildly unrealistic.

Then again, maybe I was being hard on myself. I was still in high-school, working with a distinct disadvantage for someone determined to compete on a national level. Sure, I had access to the school track, a coach, team, and equipment—but except for the track, all would vanish at the end of the school year. I now had a new pair of feet, but no way to fully take advantage of them. I needed help.

Once again, educator Susan Hall came to the rescue. "Tony could have spent his life accepting his limitations by just getting by," Ms. Hall later said. "Instead, with true grit, he made something of his life. Helping him out was the least I could do."

But she did more than just "help out"; she became my "life" coach. For one thing she pushed me into competition against other amputees. I am a *congenital amputee*—which means "from birth." Without Ms. Hall, I would never have gotten as far as I did. Not only did she arrange for me to work with Mark Schone, the physical therapist, she introduced me to a friend of hers named Julie Rowe. A teacher at Meadowdale High School, a rival high school of mine, Rowe had also been coaching their school's track and volleyball for nearly three decades. Julie was in her late forties, and had a dry sense of humor; she never wasted a word.

Later, she would tell me that the first time she saw me at a school meet, running on the cinder track, jolting along on what looked like a pair of stilts, she felt a sense of "wonder."

She said my situation offered a coach many new variables and exciting challenges. But she admitted that if we were going to succeed, "We're going to have to learn from each other, because I've never trained anyone without feet before."

And that's what we did. Five days a week in the summer we met at the high-school track for two hours, rain or shine. Usually it was just the two of us, with a lone jogger occasionally circling the track as I trained. When it rained, she coached from under an umbrella, as I got soaked. "If you really want to defeat Dennis Oehler," she said, "you must work harder than anyone who's ever lived."

Hence, she pushed me, and pushed me.

"I don't think that it is Tony's disability that calls people's attention to him," she later said. "It's his personality. You kind of get sucked in. If he'd been a surly kid with a chip on his shoulder, I wouldn't have worked with him. But he was so enthusiastic, so motivated, that it wasn't work for me at all. It was time consuming, obviously, but I loved doing it, and it surely paid off."

She coached me without charge. I would have been happy to pay her, but my folks couldn't afford it.

Chapter 8

No Hands, No Feet, No Limitations

My junior year in high school rolled around and soon it was time for another track season. My brother Art decided not to return. "You're fine on your own, Tony," he said. "It's my senior year and I want to enjoy myself—which does not include aching lungs, cramps and sore leg muscles." Art had stuck by our deal and I didn't really need or expect him to stick around.

In the locker room, one of our top sprinters said, "Hey Tony. I'm surprised to see you came back for more."

"Why wouldn't I come back?" I questioned.

"No offense, Tony, but you finished dead last in every race last year. It seems like a lot of work for nothing," he said, obviously not understanding my motivation.

"I'm back because I look forward to coming to this track where I can say 'I know you and you and you.' That means a lot to me," I told him. "You are all my teammates and friends."

And they were; we had all bonded through all the sweat and side stitches. No one ever complained about my being on the team. No one ever made fun of me or mimicked me. No parents demanded that Coach Anderson drop me from the team. I was not an imposition or an impediment. I didn't slow anybody down or cost the team any points.

I was just another athlete to Coach Anderson, just another runner he was trying to help get a little quicker out of the starting blocks. His initial dread, pity, or annoyance with this kid on his team *sans* hands and feet had evaporated. In fact, I'd added something of intangible value to the team. Having a non-able-bodied athlete on the squad proved that this team and school were not insensitive to the disabled, and that winning, though important, was not everything.

Coach Anderson later told me that he simply stopped seeing what was missing. "After the initial shock, you became just another kid running track."

Actually, Mr. Anderson didn't completely forget. My gait was still anything but normal. Next to other runners, I was conspicuously out of step, so to speak. But, as I slowly, steadily, and doggedly improved my running times, my lack of appendages stopped dominating the relationship between athlete and coach. Mr. Anderson's focus moved from "How am I going to train this kid?" to "What are you going to do next?"

"It's like Tony forgot that he had limitations," Mr. Anderson said in an interview later. "It was how Tony projected himself. If a person projects themselves as having no limitations, then other people start seeing him that way. And so they did."

And now, along with my grit and determination, I had my new Flex-Feet. I walked down the hill to practice with a new bag slung over my shoulder. Nobody paid much attention to me as I went about my normal business. Then, like a child with a secret, I slowly opened my bag while grinning slightly, and pulled out my new prosthetics.

As I started to put them on my teammates started to take notice.

By the time they were both on I was surrounded by a group of kids. As I stood up they all looked in disbelief—

My Flex-Feet made me grow about two inches—I was now taller than almost everyone on the team. Grinning from ear to ear, I walked over to Mr. Anderson and announced, "I'm ready to start practice coach!"

After he watched me run with them, Coach Anderson was stunned. "It's the difference between night and day," he proclaimed.

In sprinting, it's critical that the runner be able to both push and pull their way down the track. For so many years I had only been pushing because I had no toes. But now as my "feet" struck the ground, I was able to paw at the track, finishing each stride by pulling myself with my hamstrings.

Flex-Foot changed my life as a runner. Suddenly, track was no longer just a grin-and-greet outing, a chance to make friends. Winning was now a distinct possibility. It was well within my grasp.

While people may have thought it was the technology that allowed me to run so fast, in reality it allowed me to train harder, and it was the training that helped me go faster. It's not like I strapped on rockets that propelled me down the track. The blades were simply the closest thing to a human foot that I could have.

By my senior year, 100 meters was passing beneath my feet in the low 12-second range. My times were significantly altered. For instance, sophomore year these were my best finishing times: 100 meters, 14.38 seconds; 200 meters, 31.08 seconds. Junior year: 100 meters, 12.6 seconds; 200 meters, 26.7 seconds. Senior year: 100 meters, 12.0 seconds; 200 meters, 24.6 seconds.

Just after graduation in the same summer I ran the 100 meters in 11.65 seconds and 200 meters in 24.24 seconds; both were unofficial world records but both qualified as national records for my class. Although I was technically a "double below the knee amputee" (the word "amputee" applying equally to both those who lost a limb and those born without one), I always ran in the division for "single amputee below the knee," known in Paralympic jargon as "T44." And, astonishingly, I was not only winning there, I was beating able-bodied athletes in school meets as well.

And as I got faster, for the first time I was actually earning points for my team. I was no longer a mere curiosity. I actually had value for the team and I earned a varsity letter—I was a real jock. And my reputation began to grow.

"I have to tell you, Tony," said Coach Anderson. "After watching you cross the finish line while the winner was on his way to the locker room for so many meets, I am thrilled to see kids straining to catch *you*." I beamed. There was no way to describe the satisfaction and exhilaration of becoming the equivalent of an able-bodied athlete.

Things had changed for sure. As runners settled in the starting blocks, they'd glance over at me. They'd stare at the black carbon graphite blades strapped to my legs and attached to spiked track shoes. I'd wonder what they were thinking. Probably, "What the heck are those things?"

I was usually third or fourth out of the blocks. Before my blades, I would have dropped further and further behind. Now, midway through the race, I'd fire my afterburners and begin to reel in the leaders as I flew by most of them. People young and old started coming to the meets to watch me compete. I'd hear them yell, "Go, Tony, go!" That would give me an extra boost of confidence.

My renown in the school and around the city grew. First, there was a feature story in the town's weekly newspaper. Then reporters from Seattle's television stations and daily newspapers came to see and report for themselves. Cameras at meets were aimed at me.

Eventually, my story drew national attention. Within a couple of weeks, reporters from CBS's *48 Hours* and ESPN wanted to interview the runner without hands and feet. Only three years earlier I was hiding in a classroom eating lunch alone. Now I was the school's celebrity.

"I was trying to see if this was going to affect the way he behaved," Coach Anderson would later say. "A lot of times, when a kid gets attention like that, he starts acting differently. It goes to his head. He develops an inflated, obnoxious ego. Tony never behaved like that. He remained humble and grateful."

Humility is a constant companion when you're born without hands and feet. It's hard not to feel cursed. Yet ironically, I went from being pitied, to envied.

Coach Anderson later recalled that there was some minor resentment among a few of the kids on the team. They too wanted attention, to get their photos in the paper. I had never heard any rumblings of this so I guess I was well guarded from it. The majority of my teammates, however, respected me and were delighted to see me shining in the spotlight.

While I never experienced the thrill of being the first to cross the finish line in a high-school track meet, I had a few seconds and lots of thirds and fourths.

Once, however, I did come very close.

I was at a meet on Bainbridge Island. I was in the 200-meter race and as I rounded the curve in the lead, my teammate Max Babb was close at my heels. Everyone said it was better to run curves at 80 percent, but I figure why not run them at 100 percent? Down the final straightaway, Babb and I were running neck and neck, stride for stride. Moments later, I crossed the tape, elated. I was sure I had edged him out. It was a photo finish.

As we walked back to cool down and hear the results, I looked over at Babb. A big grin swept across his face. He'd just heard;

he'd beaten me by less than 1/100th of a second. I couldn't believe it. I was a cat's whisker away from winning a high-school track race against able-bodied athletes.

I did beat Babb a few times later that season, but only for second or third place. Our times of 24 seconds in the 200 meters weren't fast enough to win. However, our good-natured competition brought us close together. He and I remained good friends after high school. While I pursued a career in track, Babb signed up for the Marine Corps.

At the end of my high-school track career, I had realized a dream and made an important discovery. Not only did I make a lot of new friends, I discovered that I was a gifted runner.

Being a runner was an innate feeling for me, and yet it was also a way to belong, to make friends, to be liked. But after I got my first set of Flex-Feet, the sheer desire to run was all that mattered. Whenever I pictured myself running, I didn't see myself flying down the track without hands or feet. I saw myself flying down the track to beat the clock and better my own time.

My training regimen still included lifting weights. One evening while my brother and I were working out at Bally's we were approached by Jerry, a personal trainer I knew well, who started talking about Arnold Schwarzenegger. Of course, at the time Arnold was often a subject of discussion in gyms around the world. I had always respected him. He might have been cocky and arrogant back when he was competing, but he'd also shown unflappable confidence in himself. I appreciated how he adopted the concept of mind over matter and actually predicted many of his life accomplishments before ever visiting the United States. For these reasons I identified with him, and everyone at the gym knew it.

So when Jerry asked if I was going to go down to the University of Washington to meet Arnold, I thought he was teasing me. He insisted Arnold was going to be at the Hec Edmundson Pavilion the upcoming weekend. I asked how on earth he could know that. He reminded me that Arnold was very active on the President's Council on Physical Fitness and Sports, and was currently touring the country to meet with the governors of each state. The upcoming weekend would be Washington's turn.

Finally convinced, I wondered how I could pull off meeting another of my childhood idols. I wasn't alone: the three of us decided that someway, somehow, we would do it.

As it happened, my family had always been well-connected in politics. During a field trip a number of years earlier to the Capitol in Olympia, Governor Booth Gardener had entered the main room that he used when addressing members of the state legislature. I was sitting in his seat when he opened the door. As he poked his head in the room, knowing full well it was full of sixth graders, he said "Hey Tony! Please say hello to your grandfather for me."

Now, six years later, Arnold was to be meeting with the same governor.

Instead of three of us driving down to Seattle on Saturday morning there were five: Jerry, two of my brothers, a nephew and me. We had no real plan, no angle to play. All we had was the knowledge that Arnold Schwarzenegger would be at the university.

We arrived to find ourselves in chaos. We had to drive a mile off campus just to park. During the long walk back I thought hard about how to get into the room with Arnold and Governor Gardner.

When we arrived at the pavilion I turned to the rest of my gang and said, "Just follow me, guys." I led them to a line of six to eight college students waiting to check into the sports complex. We lined up behind them, and more students filed in behind us.

When it was our turn I walked up to the booth and said to the attendant, "Hello, I'm here to meet with Governor Gardner and Mr. Schwarzenegger."

She looked around to make sure nobody else heard me. "How did you hear about that?" she asked in a low voice.

I shrugged. "I was told to just come to you and ask where we are supposed to go."

She leaned forward and whispered, "Just walk down that hallway and take a right, then follow the corridor all the way down and enter the last door at the end."

I thanked her and we quickly departed down the hall. As we rounded the corner at the end we were amazed to see not only how long the second hallway was, but also that there was nobody around. I started to get a little worried. There was no activity, no security, nothing. But as we got closer to the door at the end of the second corridor we heard a commotion emanating from behind it. At the plain, unguarded door, we all paused and looked at each other as if to say, *Are you ready for this?*

My brother Mike opened the door into a different world. People walked briskly back and forth; groups huddled together, talking excitedly. There was a sense of electricity in the room. I looked around and identified the person I believed to be the event coordinator.

I maneuvered toward him, dodging and weaving through the crowd, and finally tapped the gentlemen on the shoulder. He briefly acknowledged me before turning back to stare at his clipboard. Refusing to be brushed off, I tapped his shoulder again. This time he whirled and said "*Yes*, can I help you?"

"I have something I was supposed to present to Mr. Schwarzenegger and Governor Gardner," I said, "and was told to talk to you." My "presents" were actually a couple of signed action shots of me running. The coordinator asked my name and turned back to his clipboard. "I'm sorry, I don't see you on the list and we have a very busy schedule." He walked away.

I felt rejected. Had I gotten this far only to come up short? Would it be enough for me to just be in the same room with Arnold? As I sorted through these questions in my head the room exploded with excitement. Arnold and Governor Gardner had just entered. Just as quickly as the crowd had jumped with excitement it came to a standstill as the two made their way through the room. They walked right in front of me; I could have reached out and touched one of my heroes.

I watched as Arnold interacted with some of the children who had come to meet with him. It was a media frenzy. Cameras were everywhere! Then someone grabbed my arm and started pulling me toward the front of the room. I looked over to see the event coordinator with a firm grasp of my arm. "Stay close!" he said.

Before I had time to process what was happening I broke through the crowd at the front of the room and found myself looking back at a sea of cameras and bright lights. Standing next to me with his arm extended to shake hands was Arnold Schwarzenegger.

I was in shock. I handed Arnold the envelope containing his signed photo. He took a moment to look at it and then turned to the cameras while putting his left hand on my right shoulder. "Now here," he said, "is a classic example of someone who could have taken the easy road and been a couch potato. But instead he has taken his disability and turned it into his strength!"

The media loved it. Then I was escorted over to Governor Gardner. He asked how my grandfather was and said to say hello, just like he had during that trip to the capitol years earlier.

Later I again approached the event coordinator and asked him if it would be possible to get Arnold to sign a few items we had brought. He didn't make any promises, but as he left the room,

Arnold, seeing the items in his arms, looked back at me and gave a thumbs-up. After a few minutes his assistant handed me back the items I had given him. They were all signed.

Confidence. Determination. Perseverance. Mind over matter. Features I admired in others and had worked to develop in myself—and features I would soon need, because I was about to once again face off against the man on the poster, the man with the world records, the gold medals, the fame and fortune: Dennis Oehler.

Chapter 9

The One to Beat

The USA/Mobil Outdoor Track and Field Championships is a very high-profile event. That year—1991—the Athletics Congress National Track Championships would for the first time include an amputee exhibition…and I would be participating in it.

Two weeks after graduating from high school I found myself on Randall's Island in New York City along with most of the biggest names in my sport…including Dennis Oehler. I was eager to run against him again. Despite my pledge to myself, I had placed second to him the summer before in my first senior division race at the USAAA National Championships in Bowling Green, Ohio, where I ran the 100 meters in 12.6 seconds and the 200 meters in 26.7 seconds.

The Randall's Island event was quite a spectacle. I had previously witnessed a meet of this caliber only on television—actually being a part of it was mind-blowing. Media presence was everywhere—newspaper reporters and photographers, and television crews everywhere. There were hordes of fans coming to see the top athletes in track and field. Olympic gold-medalist Carl Lewis was there.

I had a photo on the desk in my bedroom of Oehler and Lewis running side by side. It is one of the photos I had hanging in my dorm room at Hofstra University to give me inspiration during the meet in New York City in 1989. Every day I would look at it and imagine myself in the ad rather than Oehler. That was a fantasy, but being here with both of them in attendance was a dream come true.

As I prepared for a 100-meter exhibition race against Oehler, I noticed someone down toward the end of the 100-meter straight also warming up. He was an able-bodied athlete, African-American, chiseled and fast as a gazelle. I got a closer look and I realized it was none other than Carl Lewis himself! I decided to push my next wind sprint down the track a little further, timing it to when Lewis would be coming toward me. We then ran right past each other. When I turned around to walk back, Lewis was doing the same. As we passed each other, we made eye contact. He nodded and smiled. I was too much in awe to even say hello.

Someone later told me that when Lewis was on the track he usually never broke his concentration; he was always all business. To get this kind of acknowledgment, no matter how seemingly small, was very special. I felt honored—and elated.

Not long after it was time for the 100 exhibition to start. This event was an ideal showcase for Oehler. He was experienced, unflappable and in his element. I was still green and somewhat star struck. I still had a long way to go up the ladder to reach Oehler. In Ohio he had beaten me in the 100 meters by almost a full second—which at that distance is an eternity. To call me a long shot in this race would be an understatement.

Although Coach Rowe and I had cut two full seconds off my 100-meter time, I had never run the distance in under twelve seconds, which put me nearly a half-second behind Oehler's world-record time. As he settled into his starting blocks in lane one, and I settled into mine in lane seven, he undoubtedly wasn't thinking about me. Why would he? He was seasoned, experienced and had not lost a race in seven years. I was just a kid with a newly inked high-school diploma, still working on my technique. At this distance, every single move a runner makes is significant. One tiny misstep could be the difference between first place and last.

Starts had been the weakest part of my race. Before Rowe became my coach, I had begun every race from a standing position—body upright, knees bent—the pose usually assumed by middle-distance runners, who don't need an explosive launch. Sprinters, on the other hand, use the "sprinter's start." They coil down with the balls of their feet planted in the starting blocks and their upper body supported on both arms. But I can't do that. Without hands, my arms aren't long enough to reach the track.

Coach Rowe insisted that if I wanted faster times, I needed to figure out how to achieve a four-point stance.

My father had come up with a simple, creative solution: he covered a pair of sealed, empty, one-gallon paint cans with thick rubber to rest my "hands" on. Now, by placing the cans just behind the starting line and a yard in front of the blocks, I could lean down and brace my upper body on the cans, positioning myself in the same stance as every other sprinter. (While I did not need to get special approval for this accommodation, some of the other amputees eventually protested that the cans were a distraction. We had the cans covered in the same material as the rubberized tracks so they would blend in, and later on I just went to simple black cans. It was never an issue again and they became acceptable.)

That solved the four-point starting position, but there was another issue. When I pushed back on each of my prosthetic feet, they bent before propelling me forward. This created a noticeable delay before I could shoot out of the blocks. This was especially problematic when I was competing against runners, like Oehler, who had one able-bodied leg to push off with. Coach Rowe and I worked hard on solving this problem, but couldn't figure out how to overcome it.

But I was not thinking about any of this as I settled into the blocks and rested my arms on my dad's paint cans. I didn't think about the sacrifices I had made and countless hours of training I had done, nor all the people who had helped me get here and were in the stands or at home pulling for me. I didn't think about my previous losses to Oehler. I cleared my mind and focused on this moment, this race.

When the gun went off, I exploded out of the blocks. For once, I found myself ahead of everyone else, except Oehler. We matched one another stride for stride down the track, arms and legs pumping as we left the rest of the pack behind. Since our lane assignments were so far apart I wasn't completely aware of how close we were. Then the unexpected happened. As we reached the halfway mark, I began to pull ahead. With every step the gap widened, until I flew across the finish line a half second ahead of Dennis Oehler!

I was in shock. Not only had I won, I had set a personal record—running under twelve seconds for the first time in my life. Moreover I had upset the world-record holder, "the face," the handsome world-class athlete in the magazine ads!

I could only imagine what Dennis Oehler must have felt when he realized I had beaten him. Catching his breath, he looked dazed, surprised at the results. I walked back, acknowledging congratulations from the other competitors, and extended my hand. "Good race," I said. He shook my hand but didn't respond—he didn't even look at me.

"I don't know how to feel," I told the reporters during interviews just off the track immediately after the race. "Ask me when I wake up."

Although our times were wind-assisted, I finished with an official time of 11.74, my personal best by nearly half a second. Oehler's time was 12.46, but he wasn't ready to concede. It was an aberration, an anomaly, an outlier. He told a reporter in his post-race interview that the race was just a fluke. Then, in his best Arnold Schwarzenegger *Terminator* voice, he said, "I'll be back."

He was mistaken. I would never lose to him again.

That's not to say our rivalry was over—far from it. In fact, in important ways it had just begun. I hadn't really anticipated what losing would mean to a man like Oehler, nor what an off-the-track dogfight this would become. But I was about to find out.

The problem, as it turned out, wasn't really with losing on the track...it was with losing in the marketplace. There are between 350,000 and 400,000 leg amputees in this country, who spend about $500 million a year on prosthetics. So it's a pretty big business.

Manufacturers used to sell their products only to doctors and prosthetists, but not anymore. They now market them directly to the public—and the top single-leg amputee athletes are in demand and well paid to make the sales pitch.

With his outgoing personality and good looks, Oehler had lots of commercial appeal. He earned money from numerous endorsements and from motivational speeches. He'd even produced a workout video for amputees.

It must have taken superhuman determination for Oehler to have risen from the anguish of losing his leg and thus his soccer career to an entirely new athletic career where he had dominated for so long. However, as with any athlete, his endorsements and speaking engagements hinged on performance—on winning—so my beating him was a very real threat to him on an economic level.

The USA/Mobil Outdoor Championships would mark the beginning of my career as a professional athlete. In a span of 11.74 seconds, I had gone from being just another challenger to the one to beat.

The rest of that year there was only one big event, the United States Organization for Disabled Athletes Victory Games/Paralympic Trials in New York, in which I won both the 100 and 200 meters, running 11.65 seconds (wind-aided, unofficial world record, new US record) and 24.24 seconds (wind-aided, unofficial world record, new US record). The other good news about this, of course, was that I was now qualified to go to the Paralympic Games in Barcelona, Spain, in the summer of 1992.

The next major event was in 1992 at the National Handicapped Sports Amputee Games in Atlanta where I again won both events, running 11.76 seconds and 23.70 seconds (unofficial world record, new US record).

I also ran in what are called "all-comers" meets around the Seattle area as I prepared for Barcelona. These were meets where anybody could enter at any age. I ran in the adult division and was the only amputee who competed against all able-bodied runners. These were more like the high school meets I was used to.

My thoughts, however, were focused on Barcelona. After my performances in New York and Atlanta I knew that with laser-precise focus I would have a real shot at breaking two world records and winning two gold medals. I already had the support system in place, now I just needed to put in the work on continued training.

Participating in these games would not only be a dream come true, but an honor. Most members of my family, including my mother and father, had served in the military. They were very proud of their service and it was talked about often as I grew up. Since I was not eligible to serve our great country in the same way, I felt that running in Barcelona would be my way to represent the USA.

Chapter 10

The Push

For any track and field athlete there is one competition that is the pinnacle of success—the Olympics. We've all grown up watching the Games on television: the pageantry of the teams from all across the globe parading into the stadium for the opening ceremonies; the excitement of the events themselves, where a thousandth of a second can mean the difference between standing on the medal platform, or resolving to do better in four more years.

In September 1992, I found myself living that dream, and in a city worthy of dreams. The moment I stepped foot off the plane in Barcelona I felt an energy unlike any I had ever felt before. The ancient cathedrals and cobblestone roads made me feel so small in the grand scheme of things . . . yet here I knew I would have an opportunity to make a huge impact on the world.

One of the most anticipated track events at the Barcelona Paralympics was the 100-meter dash. I was very nervous before the 100-meter preliminaries, feeling more jittery than usual. One of the things every competitor worries about is not waking up on time. In fact, I had just purchased and tested a new alarm clock the day before the race. There is nothing worse than being disqualified for showing up a few seconds late after training for and dreaming about a race for so many years!

Leading up to these games in Barcelona I had taken part in a training camp in Boulder, Colorado, for athletes who had already qualified for the Paralympics. One session was in sports psychology. The ten of us who were in attendance sat in a circle and were asked to make predictions about our performances in Spain. When it was my turn to speak I said that I would run 11.6 seconds in the 100 meters and under 24 seconds in the 200 meters. With the words barely out of my mouth, I saw Dennis Oehler chuckle. One of the sports psychologists cleared his throat and told me that although I was encouraged to dream big I needed to also be realistic. I felt a little confused, like they had been telling us what they were told to say without really meaning it.

Now I thought back to their reactions, and focused on proving them wrong, on making my vision a reality.

The moments leading up to the prelims seemed to drag on as I strapped on my prostheses and paced back and forth, up and down the track. The size of the crowd, the level of competition… my nerves grew steadily shakier. I sized up my competition: two Australians, including one named Neil Fuller; Chang Ting Sun from China; Rob Snoek from Canada; as well as representatives from Austria, France, and another American.

Nervous or not, I won the race—but didn't break the world record. I finished with an 11.78, easily winning my heat despite a slow start.

The 100-meter finals were scheduled the next day, and I was determined that there would be no flaws or hiccups in this all-important race. I went to bed visualizing my race over and over, trying my best to relax.

The next morning I awoke to the sound of waves and a gentle breeze coming off the Mediterranean Sea. I walked out onto the balcony to take in the view and smell the fresh ocean air. The sun warmed my face. After a light breakfast, I showered and packed my bag. It could have been any ordinary day but for the circumstances.

In contrast to the previous day, I felt good, my body loose and relaxed. Everything just seemed right, in sync. As I began my walk to the bus I realized just how fresh and ready I felt. I've had plenty of other days when I felt good, but today was different, somehow magical. I felt a little more spring to my step. Maybe it was just the anticipation, but my whole body seemed to be vibrating slightly; I could almost hear a faint buzz.

As I entered the bus and put down my bag I reflected on all my days of preparation, all the long hours, all the sweat and all the tears. I replayed how I got to this stage, who had pushed me, who had believed in me. I thought about all the people I was here to represent. I also remembered those few who told me to give up, that my dreams where just simply that—dreams.

After the bus pulled up to the warm up track I gathered my bag and stepped out. Standing alone, looking up at the clear blue sky, I wished that all those who supported me and those who helped me get here could feel what I was experiencing. In that moment, I felt confident and prepared: I decided that this was the day that I would silence any doubters.

I walked down the long path and checked in. I was one of the first to arrive and was told I had three hours to warm up and get ready for my event. I proceeded to the first staging area, the warm-up track. The first order of business was finding a quiet spot, away from others, to mentally prepare.

I lay down next to my bag, put my arms across my forehead and closed my eyes. I heard the sounds of the city in the distance and the trees rustling in the gentle breeze. I listened to the sound of my heart beating and imagined it slowing down. I felt my body relaxing bit by bit and waited for it to tell me when it was time to start my preparations. After several minutes it happened: my mind signaled to my body that it was time. Again I thought I heard my body buzzing, the energy building.

After putting on my legs, I hopped up and slowly walked down the track. The first corner came but I decided to turn around and walk back down the same side of the track. When I got back to my bag, I turned again and walked back down the track, this time continuing all the way around. After completing a lap I started a slow jog. Again I thought I heard my body buzzing, the energy building.

I began a series of warm-up drills and continued them for fifteen minutes or so and then returned to the area where I had mentally prepared. I took small sips of water, sensing it traveling through me. I remember feeling that I hadn't ever "heard" my body so clearly.

I went through my stretching routine, getting my body as limber and flexible as possible. Then it was time to really warm up. I stood up and began my wind sprints. At first the pace was fairly slow, allowing my body to prepare for the performance I asked of it. As I repeated my sprints and built in speed, I could tell my legs were begging to go faster; I resisted. It was important not to tire too quickly. I returned to my settling place and let myself relax into a state of meditation in which I ran the race perfectly in my mind.

After some time had passed I heard an announcement over the loudspeakers: it was time to proceed to the second of three checkpoints. I gathered my bag and made my way down another long path and checked in.

Then I took my preparations to a different level. My wind sprints this time were faster. I still began slowly and built speed with each sprint. Now my body was audibly buzzing. I felt a real energy flowing through me.

After a dozen sprints and other warm-up drills I returned again to my meditation. As I waited for the call to the third and final checkpoint I lay on the ground under the darkening sky and visualized my heart rate slowing until I returned to a calm and peaceful state.

Then came the final call. I had reached the last checkpoint beneath Saint Montjuic Stadium, brightly lit against oncoming darkness. Here, I had only minutes before my event. I could hear the roar of the crowd as other events went off. I overheard an official mention that the King and Queen of Spain were in attendance, and that over 55,000 people had packed in to watch the events of the evening. I had to turn all that off and focus on the business at hand, my big race.

Over the loudspeaker, I heard: "Men's T44 final call." This was it. An overwhelming calm washed over me. I felt focused and ready. I exited the tunnel into the stadium. Nothing could have prepared me for the sight and noise of 55,000 cheering fans. I was a bit overwhelmed by the size of the crowd and how much noise they made. It took me a few seconds to take it in and then refocus. Once at the starting line I had only moments to measure my starting blocks and get my "paint cans" ready. Soon the introductions began. Each runner was announced to the crowd as we were displayed on the jumbo screen. After introductions the starter called us to the blocks.

Lined up right next to me was the current world-record holder Dennis Oehler—but he wasn't ready to race just yet.

Just before the gun went up, Oehler asked for more time. He got up from the blocks and shook his legs. I expected something like this. He was known for these theatrics and I would have been more surprised if this hadn't happened. Every sport has mind games—psychological tricks that athletes try to use to their advantage. For example, when the coach of an opposing football team calls a time-out just before the place kicker attempts a long field goal. This might rattle the player just enough to make him miss the kick.

The race was delayed for nearly a minute—which might as well have been an eternity. The runners had all been ready to go; now we all had to get back into our mental preparations again—allowing for doubt and nervousness to creep in.

I got back into the starting blocks and, once again as the race was about to start, another runner requested additional time. He claimed there was a pebble in his able-bodied shoe. I smiled, not allowing myself to get annoyed or distracted. There was another seemingly interminable delay as he removed his shoe, shook out the alleged pebble, and retied his laces.

I know mind games are a part of the deal. One's psychological fitness is just as important as one's physical fitness. But on this day I felt calm, confident, and in control.

Instead of doubting myself I focused on the disabled kids at Shriners that I had spent so much time with. I knew they were watching on TV. I focused on all the support my friends, family, and my coaches had given me. I was running for them. I was going to give it everything I had—and being distracted was not in my plan.

The starter commanded, "Runners to your mark." Everyone settled in. "Set." Then it happened—a false start. Dennis used to say that he would sometimes try to anticipate the gun to get out of the blocks faster; this was one of those times. We were called back to the starting line and asked to line up again.

I didn't mind that at all. On the first start I had been caught sleeping in the blocks and didn't react well to the gun. As I said before, the weakest part of my race has always been the start. Since I can't preload the Flex-Feet my first motion is always backwards as the feet absorb the energy when I push out and then release. We were again called to the blocks to go through the starting procedure. *Boom,* the gun went off—and again we were called back for a second false start. I had felt better on this start but still thought it wasn't my best. While somewhat nerve-wracking, the false starts had actually benefitted me.

I sensed—or maybe hoped—that this third start would be the one. As the starter called us into the blocks I settled in early and awaited his command. "Set . . ." he said, as he held us longer this time, then *boom* the gun went off and I exploded from the blocks. It felt like I had a hand on the small of my back, pushing me as I thrust forward. I emerged from my "drive phase" to find myself in the lead. I hadn't even hit the strongest part of my race yet. That came next and that is where I began to pull away from the rest of the field. The other competitors faded behind me as I continued to accelerate. As I passed the 70-meter mark I knew that the gold medal was mine, but would I be fast enough to claim the world record?

I passed the finish line and looked to the stadium's jumbo screen. I saw the words that I had dreamt about: *record del mõn*—world record! I had finished the race in 11.63 seconds, one tenth of a second faster than the previous record. Oehler came in second with 12.38 seconds and Neil Fuller of Australia was third with 12.55 seconds. I had done what others thought to be impossible. I had become the fastest man in the world with no feet. The crowd roared.

I ran over to the stands and grabbed the American flag from a team coach to begin my victory lap. As I turned the final corner where the race began, I looked to the stands and picked out my dad who has pushed his way down to the front row. I ran over to give him a hug and he whispered in my ear, "I love you." I backed up and held the flag high and proud and finished my lap.

After the mandatory drug test and the interviews it was time for the medal ceremony. There are no words to describe what it feels like to be standing on the top step of the podium, hearing the "Star-Spangled Banner" play and knowing it is for you. There are times during training, during the pain, when athletes may question if it's all worth it. I can tell you that it is. The ultimate payoff is that moment, listening to that song.

After the ceremony I was given a few minutes to exit the stadium and see my family. My dad, brothers Art and Mike, my grandfather, the family priest and my high school friend Julie and her mother were all there to greet me with hugs, kisses and high fives. Then I noticed my mother standing quietly by herself, tears running down one cheek. I walked over and put my arms around her. She whispered in my ear, "Did you feel the push?"

I pulled back and looked at her, astonished. "I wasn't ever going to mention it because nobody would believe me but yes, I did feel the push!"

She explained that just as I was lining up for the third and final start she asked my grandmother, who had passed away before these games, to push me out of the blocks. To this day that story still gives me goose bumps!

After the race, Oehler had said to reporters: "I don't want to take anything away from the kid, because he trained hard and ran a good race…but there's no way we should be in the same race. I've got one prosthesis and I do the best I can with it. Volpentest actually has an advantage because he runs with two. I guess I'll just have to chop off my other leg and get myself a second one so that next time I race I can be seven feet tall, too. I mean, that's what it's coming to, isn't it?"

Of course, he was exaggerating. I'm six feet tall and only gain two inches with my prostheses on.

So, my classification remained a minor distraction even in my moment of triumph. As I mentioned previously, I am a double below the knee amputee, who had chosen to—and had the right to—run in the single below the knee amputee division. I had no unfair advantage, especially since I have no able-bodied foot with which to push off in the starting blocks as Oehler did. Flex-Feet simply allowed me to run as if I was running with normal feet.

I chose to run in the least handicapped leg category—which was the single-leg amputee classification—because it had the fastest competition. Usually, I was the only competitor with two prostheses. And I was *always* the only one without hands. I didn't win just because of technology. It's not like I was strapping on pogo sticks or rockets. And, of course, Oehler was also using a Flex-Foot.

Coach Rowe said I won for the same reason Carl Lewis and Michael Johnson won: I had God-given talent.

The morning of the 200-meter preliminary heat, one of the coaches who had attended the Paralympics training camp in Colorado approached me. He said that he knew I had it in me to break the world record but that I should hold back a little in the preliminaries and reserve some energy for the finals later that night. Not knowing better, I agreed. But as I warmed up I felt even better than I had during my warm ups for the 100-meter final. I used the same routine, but today I just felt looser and lighter. Maybe it was having the pressure of the 100- meter race off my back, or maybe it was just the energy of Barcelona, but today I knew I would be breaking another world record.

After warm ups were complete I heard the last call for the 200-meter prelims. Again I gathered my bag and paint cans and started out the tunnel. The crowd was smaller and therefore not as loud. The atmosphere was much more relaxing. I got around to the starting line and set up my cans. After a few practice starts the introductions began and it was time to race. "Runners to your mark . . . set . . . *boom!*

The gun went off and I erupted from the blocks. Not my best start, but decent. Oehler was with me. As I came up from my drive phase I was completely relaxed. As I rounded the corner I picked up momentum and entered the straightaway not even thinking about the other runners. Confident I was securely in the lead and with about 60 meters still left to run I shut it down. I glided swiftly over the finish line and looked up at the board to see my time. To my surprise I saw 23.97 seconds—breaking Oehler's world record by four-tenths of a second!

I turned back toward the finish line with a little grin on my face and exited the track. I was greeted by the same coach who had talked to me earlier in the day. He asked, "What were you thinking?"

"I did hold back," I replied. "That wasn't full speed."

After a few hours of down time, and a leg massage in the athlete's village, I headed back to the stadium to prepare for the finals. As I began my warm-ups I stayed relaxed but also felt an energy building up inside me again. This time it was even more intense than before; like swinging a rope faster and faster and faster, feeling the velocity reach the point where I might not be able to control where the energy went when I released it. But I didn't fight it; I let it continue to build.

I went through the first, second and third staging areas. I didn't notice the others around me. My thoughts were only on my race. This time I was racing the clock and not concerned about the other athletes. Sitting in the third staging area I heard the roar from the crowd—the stadium had filled up for the night's events. The energy that had been growing inside me began to accelerate. I gripped it tight and got ready to let it loose. Finally came the announcement to go out to the track.

Again there was a full house. Walking around to the starting line I remained focused on me and the clock. Oehler and I didn't talk to each other as we prepared. I set my blocks. I took just a couple of starts to make sure I was lined up correctly.

We were announced to the crowd. This time, however, I was introduced as the world-record holder. The commands began, "Runners to your mark." I settled into my blocks and restrained the energy still growing within me. "Set!" I felt the energy that had been building begin to swell. *Boom!* The gun went off and I surged out of the blocks like a lion seeking his prey, Oehler slightly in front of me.

As I transitioned from my drive phase I began to pull away. Within the first 30 meters I had already made up the stagger on the outside lanes. Then as I came around the corner into the straightaway, something unexpected happened. I felt that energy that was building release and I hit a gear I didn't know I had. I entered the straightaway with more speed than I had ever experienced before. I was afraid my legs wouldn't be able to keep up but I remained calm and just let my body go. I knew the record that I had already set would fall tonight, but as I finished the race and looked to the clock I never would have imagined this time: 23.07 seconds! I had smashed my own world record by almost a full second!

All the seemingly obsessive adjustments to my prosthetics—which had taken several months to perfect at the Shriners Hospital in Portland, Oregon, just prior to coming to Barcelona—had paid off. It wasn't even a race. I won the 200 meters by 2.68 seconds over runner-up Neil Fuller of Australia. Dennis Oehler had finished a distant third.

I spotted my dad in the crowd. I jogged over to him and we embraced. "I love you," he said again with tears in his eyes.

Moments later, weak-kneed from the excitement and draped in the American flag, I took my victory lap, soaking in the crowd's congratulations and admiration. Halfway around the track, I nearly fell down because I was so giddy. But there was no way I was not going to finish that victory lap. I took several deep breaths and steeled myself. Waves of people rose as I passed each section. I wanted to bottle up this moment of triumph and exhilaration.

Later in the locker room, Oehler exploded. "One hell of time to learn a lesson," he yelled at himself several times, his tirade continuing for nearly a minute. I wasn't sure what he meant by that. The locker room was in stunned silence. Then he snatched up his bag and stormed out.

When it was time for the medal presentations I looked up at the big screen as they replayed my race. I was able to see what I had felt—and it was awesome.

Among the thousands of faces in the roaring crowd was my older brother, Mike—who was mouthing something I couldn't quite make out. I smiled back at him then realized what he was saying: "You flew," he mouthed, flapping his arms like a bird. My brother Art stood next to him, nodding in agreement. I gave them the thumbs-up. Chills ran through my body. I now had two gold medals, had broken the world record, and then smashed it again on the same day. It was the greatest moment in my life up to that point.

My mission was accomplished. I emerged from these games as the fastest leg amputee in the world. Nobody had never run as fast with no feet.

My final event at the Barcelona games was the 4x100-meter relay. In relay races, often people who are your fiercest rivals become your teammates and you need to switch into a different mindset—winning for the common good. Dennis Oehler, being a fellow American, was now my teammate. He would lead off the relay and I would bring the team home.

By the time I took the hand-off from my teammate Dana Jaster, the Australian team already had a five-yard lead. However, I misjudged the handoff a bit. When Dana shoved the baton under my arm, I couldn't feel it. Dana screamed at me to go and I took off, but, not really sure the baton was still under my arm, I ran with only one arm swinging. It was an awkward running style. Nonetheless I was quickly closing the five-yard gap as we raced down the final stretch to a photo finish.

Australia won in 45.95 seconds. The U.S. team was second with a time of 45.97 seconds. That's a difference of two hundredths of a second. I had considered diving across the finish line. If I'd done it, we probably would have won.

My team was disappointed, but the near comeback was exciting for the fans.

In the locker room after the race, everyone was happy except me. I was upset about the baton and how it probably cost us the race. When we practiced for the exchanges we were given a baton that was capped on both ends. Then, in the actual race, Dennis was given a normal baton that had openings at both ends. This was the type I was used to from high school. Before the race started Dennis had tried to get my attention by looking through the baton down the straightaway, where I was waiting. I didn't know what he was trying to tell me. When I got the baton I wasn't sure if it was under my arm because it was much lighter than the practice baton. Dana had even tried yelling to me when he put it under my arm that it was open on the ends and that I could run with it pinched between my fingers like I had done so many other times before. Had I known that, I could have run my normal way and we would almost have certainly won the gold.

We all rehashed this in the locker room. Nobody blamed anybody, we just couldn't believe that for no apparent reason we had been given a hollow baton—especially since the officials had indicated before the event we would be racing with the same type of baton we had practiced with.

Despite this disappointment, over the next few days I was able to relax and spend time with my family and friends and support other athletes by watching their competitions.

Then, before I knew it, the 1992 Paralympic Games were over. The 3,500 athletes from 116 countries left for home, bringing with them their medals and memories.

But there were other prizes to be won…and not all on the track.

Chapter 11

Cupid, Costco and Joltin' Joe

When I was sixteen, I was on a Seattle afternoon television program. The host asked me if I dated and what I thought about girls. I found myself put on the spot but I didn't flinch. I answered him honestly. "Girls sometimes look at me and are a little shocked and afraid, but I don't let that bother me," I told the television host, half lying. "As long as there are one or two girls out there, or even just one, that's all I need. Just one."

The problem was finding "just one." Where was she? Was she a thousand miles away or just around the corner? Would I meet her next week or the next decade? Would there ever be a special girl who would spend a lifetime with me?

In high school I rarely dated. I did, however, go to the senior prom. My lovely date was a freshman named Julie. Her sister Lisa was in my class and that's how I got to know her. After my notoriety on the track, our date became a "human-interest story." A reporter and cameraman from a Seattle television news station, which had covered my races, showed up. We all squeezed into a rented limousine, with video rolling.

"Tony is really sweet. I like him a lot," the doe-eyed girl said into the camera.

But she and I were just good friends—though she did go to Barcelona to watch me race.

It was after I returned from Barcelona that Cupid found me a match. It happened in one of the most unromantic spots possible—among the concrete floors and towering metal warehouse shelves of Costco. I had gotten a job there shortly after the Paralympics. I worked in the department they called "majors," where the jewelry counter and electronics are located. I also worked at the front door checking cards on the way in or checking receipts on the way out. I kept seeing this pretty, part-time clerk named Alison, who was a student at the University of Washington. She was tall with light-brown shoulder-length hair and a bubbly, outgoing personality.

One of my co-workers noticed I had taken an interest in her, and she in me, so he decided to help speed things up a little by playing matchmaker. He'd corner me and say, "You know, she really likes you. I think she'd go out with you." He'd take Alison off to the side and say, "I think he really likes you. I think he'd like to ask you out."

Encouraged, I begin seeking her out during breaks. We'd talk about school, of course. I also had a lot of customers who would recognize me, and that would lead to conversation about what I had done on the track. Alison was pursuing a degree in chemistry, so she had brains to go along with her good looks. Because of this, she didn't have time to watch TV so when we first met she had no idea who I was.

After a couple of weeks I decided to ask her out. When the moment came, of course, I was panic-stricken. What if she said no? Why would she go out with me? She could have just about anybody. I had felt nowhere this nervous running in the Paralympics; I was shaking.

It didn't help that a crowd of co-workers had gathered to watch. Somehow I get the words out.

"Would, ah, would you like to go out with me?" I stammered.

To my surprise, she said yes.

On our first date I took her to Bram Stoker's *Dracula*, a fatuous goose bump flick that would not rank high in Alison's consciousness as one of her favorites.

But we had fun. Only a few days passed before our second date. I had never met anyone like her before. Part of it was acceptance. Alison wasn't distracted by, preoccupied with, or hung up over my not having hands or feet. She was actually curious—and even fascinated—about my situation. She touched my arms and did not pull away. Her attitude seemed to be: "There, but for fortune, go you or I." She peered into my eyes with the warmest of smiles. She was not on a pity mission. She genuinely cared for me. I was afraid to believe and trust it at first, because I didn't want to be crushed if I was wrong, but it seemed that we were falling in love.

From the start, Alison was able to see what I had, not what I was missing. It helped that she observed me working, interacting with customers. She saw that I was not embarrassed, inhibited, or in any way restricted by my limitations and was drawn to that quality. She told me that she was impressed that I didn't wear prosthetic feet or prosthetic hands, and that I didn't attempt to disguise my disability. She was also drawn to my lack of pretense and admired my honesty and courage.

I could hardly believe my good fortune at having found her.

We became inseparable. But I was in uncharted territory as far as romance was concerned, and worried that at some point she might change her mind about me, and find an able-bodied man more attractive. I was afraid that one day she would simply vanish.

Poof! Just like that. I had dated a girl named Melissa for about three months before I went to Barcelona. We met at the Shriners Hospital in Portland, Oregon, and she lived just over the river in Vancouver, Washington. She was my first crush and first kiss. But I found out that she had been seeing someone else after I left Portland and returned to Mountlake Terrace.

My motto has always been: "High hopes, low expectations." However, with women, it was: "No hope and no expectations."

Now I actually had hope. I so wanted to believe that Alison wanted a relationship with me, and me alone.

About six months after we started dating, we were attending a Shriners function and someone asked me, "Is this your beautiful wife?"

"No, my girlfriend," I responded.

The man said, "Well, you better not let this one get away. You better pop the question soon."

I'd never dared bring up the subject of marriage with Alison.

Later that evening, however, I received a big shock. Alison turned to me and said, "Well?" I didn't even *have* to ask.

After a two-year engagement we married in August of 1995, three years after our first date.

While Alison was able to see beyond my differences, her parents were another matter. They were opposed to their daughter marrying me and gave her lots of "do-you-know-what-you're-getting-yourself-into?" lectures. I am sure they thought they had her best interests in mind, but they could only focus on what I was lacking physically instead of what I could offer their daughter emotionally.

I guess it didn't help that when I first met them I had the flu and spent most of the week sniffling, sneezing, and coughing. I wasn't my usual lively self. Her parents must have thought, "Oh great, he doesn't have any hands or feet and he's dull and sickly as well."

To win them over, Alison mailed videos and newspaper clippings about my accomplishments on the track. They were somewhat impressed, seeing that I wasn't some guy on welfare, sitting around doing nothing. But they still weren't won over.

Several months before we were to be married, Alison's parents asked her to visit them at their home in Eugene, Oregon. I wasn't invited. Not surprisingly, it turned out to be their last gasp at pleading with her not to marry me. Furious, Alison left in the middle of the night and made the five-hour drive back home. She had heard enough.

Her parents refused to help pay for the wedding expenses, though they respected her decision enough to attend the ceremony and give me a chance to prove myself. They never really came around to me, which did put a strain on our marriage. Like so many other times in my life, I took this as a challenge to prove them wrong—to show them that I *was* good for their daughter and could provide a great life for her.

Alison and I had some exciting times together. My success in Barcelona brought me accolades outside the Paralympic world. In 1994 *Sports Illustrated (SI)* selected me as Old Spice Athlete of the Month, and, later that year, as its runner up for the Old Spice Athlete of the Year. In part, here's what the *SI* article said about me:

> . . . *His greatest achievement occurred at the 1992 Paralympic Games in Barcelona, Spain. His times of 11.63 and 23.07 seconds respectively are impressive by any standard, especially for someone born without hands or feet.*
> *The Old Spice Athlete of the Month is so fast he runs in the toughest division of meets for the physically disabled, against athletes*

less handicapped than he. His coach, Julie Rowe, says, "Someone forgot to tell him he doesn't have all the parts. He's the most impressive athlete I've coached in 25 years."

"If someone challenges me, saying 'You can't do that,' I always want do show them I can," he says. "If you can dream it, you can do it."

I'll never forget the look on Alison's face when this article appeared. Even though she told her parents to go out and buy a copy, she sent them one anyway—just in case. She was so proud of me.

In the meantime, I had been invited to attend a high-visibility banquet in Las Vegas, honoring and celebrating three Italian athletes, which included one of the greatest sports stars of all time. This was our first trip to Sin City. For a couple of people who didn't come from much money, it was a treat to be picked up at the airport in a black stretch limousine and transported to the MGM Grand Hotel. Unfortunately, by the time we arrived in our lovely suite, we had only a couple of hours before the black-tie dinner, so we had to rush to get ready.

I was told that I would be sitting at the head table. The event would honor two Italian titans of the sporting world...and me. Before we knew it, we were walking into a large banquet hall, full of guests seated at tables, and then suddenly we were being introduced to Joe DiMaggio and boxer Ray "Boom Boom" Mancini!

My seat assignment was right next to the less-than-loquacious DiMaggio. Chitchat was not his strong suit. We said hello, shook hands, and that was it. He seemed aloof and indifferent.

After the master of ceremonies introduced us, some children approached the table and asked DiMaggio for his autograph. Without a word, he stood up and left the room, leaving behind his disappointed admirers.

A few minutes later, he returned and took his seat.

After dinner, as we were shoveling in the last bite of *mousse au chocolate,* another group of children approached with a few base-balls to sign. Joe saw them coming and again promptly walked out.

When he returned, he stopped and whispered into the emcee's ear. The emcee then stood and announced that DiMaggio would not be available for signing autographs. If approached again, he would leave the room and not return.

I was surprised at his reaction to the children but, not being a mind-reader, didn't want to speculate about why he did this. Like the kids, I too wanted his autograph but it was obvious this wasn't going to be easy, despite our seating arrangements. Coincidentally the *Sports Illustrated* in which I was mentioned featured DiMaggio on the cover, with the title "Where Have You Gone Joe DiMaggio?" *a la* the iconic Simon and Garfunkel song lyrics.

Still, at the risk of causing him to storm out of the room never to return, I was determined to get his signature. Since the arti-cle about me was in this particular issue, I just happened to have brought along a few extra copies.

I knew I had to engineer this operation with considerable finesse. I was sitting to DiMaggio's right, and Alison was seated to my right. I turned and asked her to discreetly open one of the four copies of *SI* in her lap to the article about me. Slowly, she maneuvered one copy onto the table as I leaned forward to block DiMaggio's view. I took out a Sharpie pen and scrawled my auto-graph above the article about me.

I sat back, waiting for the right moment to strike. It never arrived. So finally, I sucked it up, turned to the preoccupied celeb-rity next to me, and said, "Excuse me, Mr. DiMaggio, I just want to say that it has been a great pleasure and honor to be seated next to you this evening. If you would accept it, I have a gift for you."

I pulled out the *Sports Illustrated,* opened to the article about me that I had signed, and slid it in front of him.

He took a moment to read it and said, "Tony, this is just great. Thank you so much for signing it. By the way, what magazine is this?"

Smiling, I didn't respond.

He turned the pages until he came to the cover. A bit non-plussed, he stared at his own photo. I was trembling. How was he going to react? Would he stand up and storm out? Had I just ruined the evening for everyone here?

DiMaggio just kept staring at the front cover. Finally, a smile crept across his face. He slowly turned towards me, nodded his head a few times, and said, "You have a few more of these, don't you?"

Smiling, I said, "Yes, sir, as a matter of fact I do."

"Put them on the table. I'll sign them."

Without hesitating, I brought out the three other copies that Alison had been harboring on her lap all evening. We watched in stunned, but delighted, silence as Joltin' Joe signed all three of my *Sports Illustrated* copies! These were the only autographs he deigned to sign that evening.

Chapter 12

Meeting Ross Perot

After I returned from Barcelona in September of 1992 I was a little lost. I wasn't done with track and field but I wanted a break and thought I should start doing all those other things that nineteen-year-olds fresh out of high school do—plus I couldn't be a track and field athlete forever. I needed to think about the future beyond that, and so I enrolled at Edmonds Community College to work toward a general business degree, and also got that part-time job at Costco. For the time being track and field took a back seat to studying and working.

About a year later I decided to start running seriously again. I missed it, and believed I might even be able to make a living from it. But to reach that level I would need financial support. Although I had secured a small monthly stipend from Flex-Foot after Barcelona, I needed to ask for more if I was to train full time. I renegotiated my contract with Flex-Foot so I could afford to not work. I competed in many local events and even a few international events, but nothing that compared to my experience in Spain. Athletically I was still at the top of my game, but I knew I had the potential for much more than just running fast. I was beginning to think about leaving a legacy, spreading a story of hope.

But first things first. It is impossible to compete at the highest levels of a sport without a coach. About six months after my return, my longtime coach, Julie Rowe, had told me that she had taken me as far as she could. She said it would be best to find another person who could take me to the next level.

In 1995 I received a call from Bryan Hoddle, who was considered one of the best high-school track coaches in the state of Washington. He lived in Olympia, about sixty miles from me. He called me out of the blue and introduced himself. After a little chit chat, he said, "I think I know of a way to help you get out of the blocks faster. There's new equipment called the Moye block that allows you to stand in a three-point stance rather than being all the way down in standard blocks."

The only problem with these blocks was that they weren't allowable in international competition for world records to count. But we continued to talk, several times over the next five months, and agreed to meet to see what he had in mind.

At this point I had been running without a coach for a couple of years. After spending a brief amount of time with Bryan I felt that he was the missing element, and with his help I could get to that next level of performance.

This all seemed fortuitous, as though it was meant to happen. While the call came out of the blue for me, Hoddle had actually been trying to reach me for a long time. His wife was watching TV one night and caught a story about me. She called her husband to come over and watch it. The TV show mentioned that I was attending Edmonds Community College. Hoddle was impressed with my accomplishments and, ever the coach, decided to track me down through the school. He called and left a message at the school office, but I never got it.

Several months later Hoddle happened to read another story about me in *Sports Illustrated* and learned that I was living in Lynnwood. He hadn't heard from me—since I never got the earlier message—but was persistent enough to call directory assistance to get my number. He still wanted to tell me about the Moye blocks.

In January of 1995 I got up the nerve to ask him if he would consider coaching me. Bryan was hesitant because of the distance between us. Alison and I remedied this by moving to Federal Way, halfway to Olympia. After that Hoddle generously coached me without pay, and never said a word about money. Luckily, I would eventually be able to remunerate him for his time and expertise.

Fade back to 1993. I had the opportunity to meet Ross Perot, the Texas billionaire who ran for president in 1992 and 1996. After the 1992 election, he came to the University of Washington to attend a rally for his organization United We Stand America. My father arranged for me to meet him backstage. There, Mr. Perot shared with me how he had drawn on my story, which he had seen on the CBS news program *48 Hours*, to help inspire a soldier who had his leg amputated after the Gulf War. As he shook my hand he said, "If there is anything I could to do help you, don't hesitate to ask."

I took that offer to heart. I had a business manager, Larry Weber, a state worker living in Olympia with a background in track at the national level. He also had a gift for defeating challenges. My coach, Bryan, was a friend of his and initially linked us up in 1995, about three months after Alison and I got married.

Larry arranged for another, more formal meeting with Mr. Perot, this time at his office in Texas and also including Bryan. Mr. Perot's office was a reflection of his patriotism. At the entrance sat a four-foot replica of the Lincoln Memorial, and Norman Rockwell prints hung on the walls.

During this meeting he asked, "What do you need to succeed in Atlanta? What can I do to help you repeat your double gold medal performance from Barcelona and defend your title on American soil?"

The answer to that was simple. I needed new, updated prosthetics; full-time coaching; assistance in getting to all of the meets necessary to help me prepare for the Games in Atlanta.

Mr. Perot did not blink. A plan was set in motion to secure Bryan as my coach. Perot offered to compensate him for his time, which benefited Bryan as much as I—it allowed him and his wife to make one of their dreams come true: adopting a child.

Mr. Perot was also instrumental in fitting me with the state-of-the-art prosthetics I required—a refinement of the idea and design of the legs the Shriners hospital in Portland, Oregon, had built for me in 1992.

Mr. Perot said, "I saw a story on *48 Hours* about this facility in Oklahoma; it's the best in the country. Now what was that name?" he asked, trying to pull it from his memory. Then he buzzed his assistant, saying "Barbara, get me Dan Rather." I tried to hide my surprise. Within five minutes *the* Dan Rather, famed CBS newsman, was on the phone but he didn't know the name off the top of his head, either. He said he would find out and call back. Not long thereafter, he called back with the name of John Sabolich.

Mr. Perot then told Barbara, "Call Sabolich and set up a meeting for today. Get these folks on the first flight over there, but they need to be back today." It was amazing to watch Mr. Perot in action. Before we knew it he flew us all to Oklahoma City in a whirlwind trip that had us back to his office in three hours.

Representatives from NovaCare-Sabolich greeted us at the airport and took us to an amazing facility. John Sabolich, the founder, was the best of the best. His prosthetics were cutting edge and he wasn't afraid to take chances and push the limits of design. When we arrived at Sabolich we were taken into a large conference room where there was a large circle of chairs with two more in the middle—one for me and the other for John Sabolich. I was introduced to all the folks in the room and then, without a pause, I found myself and my coach being bombarded with questions about what we needed. Which event was I training for? Ideas went back and forth between all the individuals in the room. After about forty-five minutes we were hurried back to the airport and within the next hour were seated back in Mr. Perot's office. As we arrived, a fax was coming in from Sabolich. Mr. Perot was ready and willing to pay for these newly proposed prosthetics but Sabolich insisted that they donate them to me.

All the pieces were coming together.

With Mr. Perot's sponsorship, I was able to train full time. I only had eleven months until the 1996 Paralympics in Atlanta. Three times a week, I drove thirty-five miles to meet with Bryan Hoddle at an all-weather high-school track.

Hoddle's initial observations were positive. He said that from my knees to my chest I was one of the strongest athletes he'd ever seen. He was impressed with my quad-to-hamstring ratio. People pull their hamstrings all the time because the usual ratio of quads to hamstrings is 80-20. Mine is about 60-40, the result of having to compensate for not having feet. A lifetime of balancing without feet had resulted in strong upper legs.

In the beginning, Hoddle went somewhat easy on me while he took a week or two to assess me. I told him to treat me like any able-bodied athlete. He took this to heart, and after the evaluation period went all out, working me full bore to maximize my strengths and minimize my weaknesses.

First he worked on my mechanics. Studying videotapes, he noticed that I had a tendency to gallop and overstride. Through repetitive drills, my running form improved. After a practice I often said, "That was the hardest workout of my life," but I was fine with that. If I wanted to break my own world records I would have to pay the piper— which I was more than willing to do.

Bryan's mission was simple: sculpt me into a sprinting machine. And that's exactly what he did. The brutal workouts—the same as he gave his elite high school athletes—continued day after day for months. He pushed me in ways I didn't think possible. As a result of his training techniques I was able to run harder and faster with less recovery time. The result of this intensity started to pay dividends quickly.

Hoddle didn't overlook anything when it came to shaving a tenth of a second off my best time. He also worked with Sabolich and his people to make tweaks to adjust my prostheses. The changes were subtle but the outcome significant. The prosthetists figured out how to reduce by two pounds the socket portion of the prosthesis into which I slipped my legs, making each prosthesis just under three pounds with the feet attached. This reduced my total weight by four pounds—which in the world of sprinting can mean the difference between first and second place. It might give me another tenth of a second edge—the margin between winning and going home disappointed.

Hoddle realized that he was dealing with a brand-new technology. We were pioneers. He said, "It's like you are the first guy traveling to Mars and back."

Coach Hoddle was also committed to enhancing the status and credibility of the Paralympics. He wanted to make a statement about our ability, using my work ethic and performance as examples. He wanted people to understand that amputee athletes train just as hard, and are just as committed to their sports, as the Michael Johnsons of the world.

After four months of training, my first race with my new legs was at an indoor meet at the University of Washington in late January 1996. I was running against six post-collegiate, able-bodied athletes. I finished respectably in the middle of the pack. Three weeks later, I raced in the Bill Cosby Invitational in Reno, Nevada, again against all able-bodied athletes in the open division. I came in an impressive second place with a 7.1 finish in the 55 meters.

People couldn't believe it. A double amputee was giving able-bodied sprinters a run for their money.

After the race, I spent close to an hour signing autographs. I also did an interview with ESPN. My reputation was growing. I was breaking barriers and proving that disabled athletes could compete with able-bodied athletes. It was amazing to see the difference between how some athletes treated me before a race versus afterward. The attitude went from, "Man I feel kind of sorry for this guy," to, "Wow, I was just beat by a guy with no hands or feet."

It was good to be back on the track again. I relished the challenges of getting back in shape and competing.

Before I could think about the 1996 Atlanta Paralympics, I had to qualify for the games. The one and only qualifying race—to get an invitation to the actual trials, where you then basically needed to prove that you were still able to represent the U.S. at the games—was held at the Massachusetts Institute of Technology (MIT) in Cambridge. I felt confident going in, but prior to the prelims of my first event, the medical staff on site who were in charge of the classifications told me I needed to be reexamined. The doctors wanted to take some measurements.

"What for?" I asked.

"There's a new rule that regulates the height you can be with your prosthetics on," said the onsite staffer, adding that this ruling came from one of the head medical officials from New York.

I shrugged. Why not? I had gone through this kind of scrutiny before and always received the nod.

But this time, after the doctors measured me, they said I was ineligible to race. They claimed I was an inch too tall.

I was flabbergasted, and trapped in a dilemma. If I raced, I'd be disqualified. If I didn't race, I'd be ineligible for the Atlanta Paralympics.

Crushed, I dropped out of the race. My chance of repeating as the 100- and 200-meter champion in the Paralympics had been struck down.

I didn't want to pay to have my plane tickets changed, plus I wanted to support the other athletes, so I stayed at the meet. The evening prior to what should have been my race, I bumped into Dennis Oehler at a meeting for all the competing athletes. He wished me good luck.

When I didn't respond, he said, "Aren't you running?"

I shook my head. "I'm disqualified based on my height."

"You're kidding," he said. "Who in the heck would have done that?"

The next day, with his main competition—ME—forced out, Oehler easily won the race at MIT.

I immediately and vigorously protested the ruling about my height. In hopes of gaining ammunition for my appeal, I consulted an onsite prosthetist and told him about the formula used to disqualify me. It involved measuring the femur from the hip to the knee and then from the knee to the ground. After he measured some of the sprinters on the MIT track team, he found that if the same formula had been applied to them, nineteen of the twenty sprinters would also have been disqualified.

I was the only participant measured prior to that race. The

restriction was so clearly created for me that it became known by all the athletes and coaches as the "Tony Rule." The only person who didn't call it this was Dennis Oehler.

Through the grapevine, I later learned that a former coach of Oehler's had called a doctor in New York—a top-ranking medical official for the games—and persuaded him to come up with a rule restricting a runner's height *and to make sure it would apply to Tony Volpentest.*

I wasn't going to just stand there like a target. While I was still at the event, I filed a formal protest with Bob Wade, a member of the Governing Board of the International Paralympic Committee (IPC), in which I included the prosthetists findings about the sprinters on the MIT track team. Wade called a special meeting at which the board determined that the formula used to disqualify me was deeply flawed and unjust, and the decision to ban me was overturned.

That was a gratifying result, of course—but in order to avoid similar challenges in the future, I decided to have my prosthetics shortened by nearly an inch.

In order to be fair, the IPC ordered that another qualifying event for the Atlanta Paralympics be designated. At that meet, even with my lowered stature, I easily qualified.

The irony is, my shorter prosthetics actually made me *faster.* Although the missing inch shortened my stride, it quickened its frequency.

But I hadn't heard the last of the "Tony Rule". A week before the Atlanta Paralympics, two doctors from Sweden insisted on measuring me to prove I was within the permitted limits. They told me the information would be to my benefit, a hedge against further protests, so I consented.

Bob Wade later told me that these same doctors promptly filed a formal protest against my height. Wade rejected their petition, telling them there'd be no further protests against me.

And so I dodged another bullet. I would be allowed to compete in the 1996 Paralympic Games.

Despite the Tony Rule fiasco, I had no lingering hard feelings toward Oehler. I gladly acknowledge the fact that he brought respectability and public attention to the Paralympics. No one can ever take that away from him. But I would much rather he had spent his time and energy competing against me fairly and honestly, on the track, and not through covert actions like this. At thirty-six years old, Oehler had to know that his best days as an athlete were behind him, and maybe that's why he went to such lengths to be rid of me. I guess I'll never know for sure. What I was certain of was that I still had a lot more racing to do, and a lot to prove to myself.

One event I raced in leading up to Atlanta was held in Houston, Texas. This race proved to be a turning point for me. In warm-ups I caught myself watching one of the other competitors. He was older but well-muscled and looked like he was chiseled out of stone—the picture of American sprinting dominance. I walked up to Bryan and said, "Are you kidding me? Have you looked at this guy?" Rumor on the track was that he ran 10.1 in the 100 meters.

Bryan said, "Hey! You're going to beat this guy!" But I knew it would take a perfect storm of events for that to happen.

We settled into our blocks and the crowd grew silent. I remembered Bryan's words, then the gun went off and the unthinkable happened—the sprinter slipped. Just as quickly, however, he picked himself up and was off. He was so fast that despite stumbling he was still in front of me. But I had developed a knack of knowing how I would place in a race within the first ten meters after the start, and my sixth sense told me that this race was mine.

We accelerated down the track with me trailing slightly most of the way. At about seventy meters I started to inch up on him. The small crowd of maybe 200 sounded louder than the 55,000 that had packed the stadium in Barcelona. And as we drew closer to the finish line they got louder still. At eighty meters I felt my body hit a gear that I had never felt before. Before I knew it I was shoulder to shoulder with this sprinting powerhouse and as we crossed the finish line I just snuck past him.

My time was 10.98 seconds, faster than I had ever run before by far. Unfortunately, since not all of the required criteria were in place my time could not be submitted as a new world record, but all of my questions about the hard work with Bryan had been answered. It was worth it and then some.

That experience in Houston stuck with me. All of my races after that point would be faster than my world record performances in Barcelona. I unofficially broke my world records in the 100 and 200 meters half a dozen times before departing for Atlanta.

In the months leading up to the Paralympics, I raced ten times. Again in Houston, a month before the games, I came up with my best back-to-back performances. I ran the 100 in 11.26 seconds and the 200 in 22.76 seconds. My expectations skyrocketed. I was learning to shut out the crowd and my competitors, and just focus on my lane.

Bryan knew that psychological training was just as important as physical preparation. He urged me not to worry about what I could not control. There was no need to concern myself with my opponents, the weather, or the crowd. Just block everything else out. It was not as easy as it sounds. It took lots of practice and I employed mental exercises, which were also exhausting.

Eight days before the Paralympics began on August 16, 1996, Hoddle and I flew to Atlanta, where I began working out at the training facility of his good friend, Loren Seagrave. Seagrave was considered one of the best sprint coaches in the world.

To escape the heat and humidity, I worked out in the mornings. During one of the sessions, I noticed some black dust where one of my Flex-Feet attached to the prosthetic socket. Hoddle immediately called NovaCare-Sabolich. The next morning, a Sabolich representative flew to Atlanta from Oklahoma City and repaired the problem. He used another laminated layer of carbon fiber in order to avoid a possible break while I was racing. I can't say I wasn't nervous—I certainly couldn't afford an equipment malfunction—but I had to push any anxiety out of my head and focus.

Back on the track, I did some wind sprints to make sure that my prostheses would hold up. I needed that peace of mind, because I wanted so badly to break my own world records in the 100- and 200-meter races.

But of course the most important pieces of "equipment" were my will and determination. Soon, I would see if my hard work would bear fruit.

Chapter 13

Staying on Top

The big day had finally arrived. It was time to make the journey from Seattle to Atlanta. This occasion felt a little different than the Barcelona games. Maybe because it was my first time competing in the Paralympics, the Barcelona games had had an almost magical quality about them. This time felt more "workmanlike". Before, I had no preconceived notions or lofty expectations. This go-round I felt a little pressure because I was the defending world-record holder and gold medalist.

I also now had Ross Perot in my corner and I didn't want to let him or anyone else down. But while more might be expected of me, I also knew that I was better prepared than I was before leaving for Barcelona. Not that Julie Rowe didn't train me well, but both my body and the technology I was running on were more mature now, and I was able to train that much harder as a result.

When I arrived in Atlanta I went to the Paralympic Village for processing. Afterward, I went to the host hotel where my business manager was able to secure a suite for me and Alison. Athletes typically have to stay in the village, but because of the amount of press around and the distractions, an exception was made for me. This allowed me more time with my wife and family, as well, which was a welcome comfort while preparing for an event of this caliber.

I had about a week before the opening ceremonies and my first event. Other than a few workouts I spent most of the time in interviews and staying off my feet. My coach and my business manager, Larry Weber, kept me focused on the task at hand.

The first order of business was qualifying in the 100 meters. The morning of my 100-meter semifinal I went through my normal routine but felt a little off. During warm-ups I didn't feel like I was able to hit my top gear. Maybe the pressure was starting to get to me. I went through all of the checkpoints as my race grew nearer. I remembered back to my experience in Barcelona. Where was that excitement, where was that energy?

Final call came and as I entered the track from under the stadium I noticed that the crowd was almost non-existent. Maybe that's why I felt so sluggish. I tend to feed off of the energy from others and there just weren't a lot people around to create that sense of excitement.

After brief warm-ups our event was called. In my semifinal I was unfamiliar with a few of my competitors. We were called to our mark. The gun went off and to my surprise there was an athlete from Australia, someone new to me, named Bradley Thomas, who darted out quickly in front of me. This caught me off guard and it took me a few moments to recompose myself and finish the race. I came in first place but my time was slower than my world record time from Barcelona. I was relieved, however, to have my first race out of the way.

Over the next few days I started to feel more like myself. I loosened up and relaxed more. The media asked all sorts of questions about why I was unable to break the 100-meter world record in the prelims. Bryan's answer to all of them was, "He is saving it for the finals." I just continued to focus and never let any doubt enter my mind. I knew I was prepared the best I could be.

The morning of the 100-meter final I sat in my hotel room with Bryan. He handed me a list he had prepared of all the good things that would happen on this race day.

- ☑ world record
- ☑ gold medal
- ☑ major press
- ☑ break 11.0
- ☑ sponsors will see performance
- ☑ no wind
- ☑ tail wind

He had circled all of them as we went through each and every item. The only one he didn't circle was number 4: break 11.0. He said I had already done that and if it happened, great, but if not, the record was still going to fall.

The one thing we didn't expect when we arrived at the stadium was a rain delay. With a wet track, record times would become more difficult. On top of that I found out that Ross Perot and his daughter were in attendance. This would be the first time that he would see me run live.

For some reason, at this point, as I stood behind my blocks and peered down the track, I felt an overwhelming peace fall over me. I stood there and actually imagined the entire race from start to finish. It was like I had TiVo'ed the race, watched it, and was now rewinding it to live it in real time.

All the runners were announced, "Runners to your mark." I was more focused than ever before. "Set." I coiled down into the blocks, arms resting on my custom paint cans, ready to explode. *"Boom!"* The gun went off and my race with destiny began.

As I pushed through the first 10 meters I stayed low and drove with my quads, then as I transitioned between my push and pull phase I found myself in an unfamiliar place. At 30 meters I was already tied for the lead. Then I had the same feeling come over me as when I was in Houston; I felt that extra gear kick in, like a jet hitting its afterburners. I pulled away from the pack and as I crossed the finish line I saw my time with the words "world record" on the JumboTron. On this wet track, in front of family, friends, my coach, my manager and Ross Perot I had managed to run 11.36 seconds and officially break my world record. Neil Fuller came in second in 11.97 and Bradley Thomas third in 12.02 seconds. Dennis Oehler came in a distant fourth with a time of 12.43 seconds, far out of medal contention.

After the race I ran over to my wife Alison who, after giving me a quick hug and kiss, handed me the American flag. I took a short victory lap up and down the 100-meter straightaway and then jogged over to the sidelines where Mr. Perot was waiting with arms stretched out. He said to me "Tony, that was great! Congratulations, I'm proud of you!"

It's hard to describe how amazing it felt to win gold on American soil. As an athlete I was representing our great country and felt so much pride to have accomplished this at home.

Six days later, it was time to run the 200 meters. On this occasion, it was not my competitors who were generating the mind games but the disorganized race officials. For reasons nobody understood, the race was delayed a half hour. On the spur of the moment, the decision was made to squeeze in my race before the marathoners arrived. They would soon be pouring into the stadium, heading for the finish line.

These things happen in sports. Since this was out of my hands I should not have allowed myself to get annoyed—but I did. I didn't have enough time to stretch and warm up. My knees felt like cement. I just knew it was not going to be my best day.

I did win the race in 23.23 seconds for my second gold medal. The runner-up, Neil Fuller of Australia, was at least 10 meters behind me and finished in 24.72 seconds. But I had fallen short of my world record time of 23.07, which I set in Barcelona. I was quite disappointed.

Because the marathon runners were now coming into the stadium, I also could not take the traditional victory lap because race officials were concerned I might interfere with them.

Later, as I was about to re-enter the stadium to receive my gold medal, Bryan pulled me aside. He knew I was disappointed, to say the least.

"I really wanted the record," I said.

"You've got what matters," my coach replied. "You're the champion."

He was right, of course, I did repeat as Paralympic champion. To top off my experience in Atlanta I was featured on the front page of the sports section in *USA Today* and CBS aired a segment soon after that shared my experiences.

The Atlanta dream was now in the books but this time there would be no two-year layoff. Bryan Hoddle would make sure of that. There was so much more to accomplish.

While this might sound trite, I am sincere when I say that I was not running just for the money and the glory. I was running to incrementally change the world. I wanted to help transform the way disabled people are perceived and the way they perceive themselves.

Slowly, the message is getting out there. The Paralympics have come a long way since 1948, when it was launched by soldiers maimed in World War II. The next big step was 1960, when it was held in conjunction with the 1960 Olympics in Rome. And onward from the 1988 games in Seoul, South Korea, the Olympics and Paralympics are in the same venues with the Paralympics held just following the Olympic Games.

The sport is growing. Approximately 3,500 disabled athletes from 127 countries competed in Atlanta over ten days, and 200 world records were broken. And for the first time, the Paralympics were televised in the U.S. on cable, and CBS showed an hour of highlights on each of the four weekend days.

I saw "What's your excuse?" posters everywhere, promoting the event.

The message was clear. Just because you're disabled, it doesn't make you different or any less of a person or an athlete.

Chapter 14

Sprinting with the Stars

After my successes in Atlanta I was pushed and pulled in all sorts of directions. The big question was: how long could I hold on to the number one ranking in the world? I had already overcome the "Tony Rule" so that wasn't a distraction anymore. The other athletes started adopting my training mentality and seeking out coaches like mine who were well-versed in producing top-quality sprinters.

I had long had a friendly rivalry with Australian Neil Fuller. He had placed second to me in both the 100 meters and 200 meters in Atlanta and was training harder than ever. In 1997, the year following the Paralympic Games, we met for the first time since the games at The Ultimate Challenge. The meet was sponsored by Flex-Foot and held at the Olympic training center in Chula Vista, California. Neil's hard work on the track paid off for him; he beat me for the first time ever in the 100 meters.

Now the rivalry really ignited. It was a healthy one with no underhandedness or ill will—just good competition.

My manager, Larry, was always on the lookout for opportunities. In less than a year he had negotiated major sponsorships with Flex-Foot, NovaCare-Sabolich and Mannatech. As a result, my annual income skyrocketed to well over $100,000.

Larry persistently called Mannatech, a publicly traded multi-national nutritional supplement company, to try and negotiate a deal for me. They said that I could give a brief motivational talk at one of their conferences in Seattle, and audience reaction would be the determining factor in whether or not I would get a deal with them. If the audience was not persuaded by my talk, Larry agreed he would stop calling.

A few weeks later, I give my little spiel to an audience of about 2,000 people. It only lasted ten minutes and I spoke about what it's like to overcome obstacles. In conclusion, I said, "If you can dream it, you can achieve it." It's been my motto all along.

The response from the crowd was thrilling. A Mannatech executive passed Larry a note. It read, "Home Run."

I became the first disabled athlete ever sponsored by Mannatech, which had on its roster former professional athletes like Bob Lilly, Tony Dorset, Leroy Burrell, and George Gervin, endorsing their food supplements.

Larry was able to open doors for the physically challenged by breaking down stereotypes. He made a powerful point. Physically challenged athletes aren't any different from able-bodied ones. There is no distinction between those running on legs versus those on prosthetics. Both require dedication, determination, and superb athletic ability.

Thanks in large part to Larry, high-profile disabled jocks like me are able to capitalize on our successes and become pitchmen for prosthetic companies, whose annual sales currently hover around half a billion dollars in the U.S. alone. And thanks to the astonishing and rapid improvements in prosthetics, there are a wide variety of options available, including materials like titanium and carbon-graphite. These improvements allow an amputee to ride a bike, play volleyball, and run. Back in the fifties and sixties, the only option was a wooden leg without a hinge at the knee.

But beyond the money, there is a higher calling. The challenges overcome by disabled athletes have offered a lifeline to anyone lacking a foot, a leg or a hand. Instead of becoming despondent and feeling defeated other disabled people might say: "If he can do it, why can't I?"

Soon after The Ultimate Challenge, Larry heard that a Canadian promoter was putting together an exhibition event in Toronto pitting top athletes against each other for the fastest-, longest-, or highest-in-the-world bragging rights. There would be a competition between the world's top two male and female athletes in the pole vault, the long and high jumps, and the hurdles. For example, pole-vaulters Okkert Brits of South Africa and Lawrence Johnson of the United States would compete. Jackie Joyner-Kersee of the U.S. would face Olympic champion Heike Drechsler of Germany in the long jump. Ludmilla Engquist of Sweden and Michelle Freeman of Jamaica would face off in the 100-meter hurdles.

These events would center around the premier event—bragging rights to the fastest man in the world. At that time, there was a fierce rivalry between Michael Johnson of the U.S. and Canada's Donovan Bailey. At the Atlantic Olympics, Johnson shattered the world record in the 200 meters, and was the first man to win the gold medal in both the 200- and 400-meter races. At the same time, Bailey had won the gold in the 100 meters by smashing the world record. Usually the holder of the 100-meter world record is regarded as the fastest man alive, but Johnson's 200-meter time had been so fast that he claimed the "fastest man in the world" title for himself.

A rare showcase for track and field, this One-on-One Challenge of Champions event was set for June 1, 1997. The promoters had a dilemma as far as what distance to use—100 meters or 200 meters—so they compromised at 150 meters.

The winner of each event would receive a Waterford crystal trophy. Adding to the hoopla would be a $1 million cash prize to anyone who broke a world record. This event hoped to draw international attention and thus would be broadcast on CBS.

Larry saw this as an incredible opportunity to highlight Paralympic competition. He envisioned Neil and me competing head-to-head in the 100 meters for the fastest-amputee-alive bragging rights.

There were two daunting questions. Would anyone care? And how could he get us a seat at the table?

Larry called Otis Birdsong, the former NBA player who was also a Mannatech-sponsored athlete and motivational speaker. Maybe his connections could open the right doors. Fortunately, Birdsong was also excited about the idea and he led us to the right place.

After months and months of persistent calls and endless negotiations with Giselle Briden, the organizer of the event and president of Magellan Entertainment Group, Larry was able to get Neil and me set up on the list of competitors.

We were ecstatic! CBS would broadcast my race across America and around the world. The CBC would do the same throughout Canada. It was an astonishing accomplishment. Despite his inexperience, Larry had pulled it off. I would take part in one of the biggest—and possibly most lucrative—track events of the year.

"A lot of prayer went into this," Larry said. "It is answered prayers that made this happen. That's who deserves the credit."

With a simple nod of Briden's head, the impossible had become a reality. There was a catch, however. Apologetically, she said that all she could offer Neil and me was $2,500 each, plus expenses, far less than the other non-showcase athletes. Johnson and Bailey would receive $500,000 each just for showing up, and the winner would pocket another $1 million.

But the money wasn't important. Heck, Neil and I would have competed for free. All that mattered was the exposure for the Paralympic movement.

I trained tirelessly to prepare for this once in a lifetime event. Neil had the momentum after beating me earlier in the year in California but I was determined to not allow him to repeat that success. Because the negotiations to get us into the race took so long, I only had a few months to prepare and not an entire year to plan and strategize like I did for the games in Atlanta. Bryan pushed me like I was preparing for the Paralympics again. I knew that breaking the world record would be tough given these circumstances but I didn't let that change my mind set. I trained with the same intensity and determination as I had for Atlanta.

Five days before the race, Larry, Bryan, Alison and I flew to Toronto. From the moment we landed, we were treated like royalty.

There was a press conference at the local Planet Hollywood. All the athletes sat at a long table set atop a stage. We each had our own microphone and nameplate. We fielded questions from members of the press as the sporting world's attention began turning toward this event. The rivalry between Neil and me was brought up. We had agreed that we would focus our efforts to use this event to project a positive image and message about what people with disabilities are capable of doing, rather than focus on our personal rivalry. Neil was a dear friend off the track and a motivator/competitor on the track.

Two days later, I was working out at the University of Toronto, trying to stay loose and relaxed before the big race. After I finished my warm-ups and stretches, my coach tapped me on my shoulder. When I looked up, I saw that Michael Johnson had just entered the track. I remember the night he broke the world record in the

200 meters in Atlanta. I stayed awake just staring at the ceiling in total shock at the time he ran—19.32 seconds. Johnson was my idol. He is to track and field what Michael Jordan is to basketball.

As he began his warm-ups, Bryan wandered over and started talking to Clyde Hart, Johnson's coach. After a few minutes he motioned me over.

"You don't have to introduce me to Tony," Johnson said, shaking the end of my arm. "I know who he is."

Hart, who was also the track coach for Baylor University, interrupted. He asked if I'd autograph some of my posters for him.

"I can't wait to hang these up at Baylor," he said. "For anyone who gets down and discouraged, this will help pick them back up. Tony, you're an inspiration for everyone."

Hart kindly added that my accomplishments in track were equal to Johnson's Olympic record in the 200 meters. Johnson nodded in agreement. I doubted if that was true, but it was nice to hear it nonetheless.

As if my head wasn't already spinning, Johnson then asked if I'd like to run a few wind sprints with him! I jumped at the chance, while trying to contain my excitement. I ran a few with him and then we each continued our own workouts.

The morning before the race, CBS's Craig Masback—who was an old friend of Larry's dating back to their collegiate track competitions against each other—interviewed me. Masback and I chatted about the usual—what it is like running on prosthetics, living without hands and feet, and making a career out of the most unlikely of all events: running.

The interview, which couldn't have gone better, was slated to run the next day, moments before my race with Neil. Just like Jackie Joyner-Kersee, I would get a couple of minutes of airtime—a minute excerpted from the interview and the twelve-second race itself. That would be my portion of the hour-long program. This was the Johnson-and-Bailey event. Everyone else was a sideshow. I understood that.

Nonetheless, it would be an incredible moment for me and the entire Paralympic movement, struggling for acceptance and attention.

That night, Alison and I attended a black-tie fundraising event, where we rubbed elbows with celebrities. One minute I was called over to shake hands with Tommy Hilfiger; the next Michael Johnson was introducing me to his parents as the fastest amputee in the world.

During dinner, the athletes were called up on stage one at a time to give a brief talk. Neil and I were the last to be introduced, but we received the biggest applause.

Neil explained how he felt after his right leg was amputated in 1989. He had shattered his shin and severed an artery during a national youth soccer match in Australia. I talked about overcoming a rare birth defect, and that I was determined never to let it prevent me from reaching the podium I was now standing on. After that, Neil and I squared off—like Mohammed Ali and George Foreman—exchanging mock punches, drawing laughter and applause.

Near the end of the evening I found Neil standing in front of the trophy case in the back of the room. He was gazing at the $10,000 Waterford crystal trophy. On it was engraved, "100-meter Paralympic Champion."

With a smirk, he turned to me and said, "This is mine."

I hated to disappoint him, but he was mistaken. I wished him the best of luck and walked away.

The following morning I went through my usual ritual of stretches in my hotel room. I ate my normal breakfast of eggs with a slice of toast and then departed for the stadium.

I was greeted by a crowd of television cameras and journalists. I felt more like a rock star than an athlete. I suppose top professional athletes go through this all the time, but this was a first for me.

After a few interviews, I headed for the track. The 55,000-seat Skydome was about half full. I begin my warm-up routine, trying to block out all external and internal distractions. I lay on my back stretching. I was doing a fairly good job until the pre-event entertainment began. The obnoxious, high-decibel roar of revving motorcycle engines erupted on the other side of the paper-thin temporary wall that separated the athletes from the track and the festivities. I heard the announcer welcome the Blues Brothers! Just on the other side of that wall Dan Aykroyd and John Goodman sat on their Harleys. After riding up to the stage they started singing "Soul Man"—a very difficult thing to block out!

When the entertainment ended, it was time for Neil and me to go head to head. Music we had pre-selected blared as our names were announced. Up on the JumboTron played a video of me in full flight, accompanied by The Shamen's "I Can Move Any Mountain."

After all the lead-up, we were ready to take to the track and settle our score. Neil's defeat of me at the meet in San Diego three months earlier had been my first loss against another disabled athlete in nearly six years. My slip coming out of the blocks had doomed me in that race, but I would make sure it didn't happen this time.

Approaching the blocks, I thought about breaking the world record, and the million-dollar bonus prize. I settled into the blocks, canceling out all thoughts and crowd noises. I focused only on the clock and the starter's gun.

"Runners to your mark." I remained fixed on the gun. "Set!" I coiled myself up like a cheetah preparing to pounce. "*Boom.*"

The gun went off and I leapt. I stayed low and pumped my legs. My start was unusually good. Neil was out in front because he can push off with his good leg. At 40 meters, I hit my afterburners and rapidly gained on him. Then for some reason, I took a longer than usual stride at a point in the track that had a slight dip. This track has been laid out directly on top of the Skydome's cement floor and it is anything but even. I grazed the track with the very tip of my right Flex-Foot and felt certain I was about to go flying head over heels. Somehow, I didn't. Within three strides, I regained my top speed. At 70 meters, I found myself neck and neck with Neil. Again, I fired my afterburners and pulled away from him, flying across the finish line.

My winning time was 11.69 seconds and Neil ran 11.77 seconds. I missed the world record by three tenths of a second. That single misstep cost me and my family $1 million. We sure could have used the money. Who couldn't? Although I won this nationally televised event, I couldn't help but think about what might have been.

A couple of hours later, the competition's final event was held—the headline Johnson-Bailey race.

Leading up to it, the two sprinters had been exchanging barbs, with Bailey especially outspoken and provocative.

Now the crowd was hushed. The two world-famous, world-record holding sprinters got set in their blocks. There seemed to be an inordinate delay. Finally, the gun went off. Johnson and Bailey burst out and shot down the track. But at the halfway point, Johnson pulled up lame, giving Bailey an easy—and less satisfactory—victory.

"It's obvious that the gap was going to get bigger and my butt was going to get smaller and smaller as I pulled away from him," said Bailey in a trackside interview right after the race. "He knew he was going to get hammered after the first 30 meters, so he knew he had to pull up to save face."

One commentator called my contest the far more exciting race of the day.

My wife phoned home to Seattle to get the hometown reaction to my race. Hanging up the phone, she looked shocked. "Your race wasn't televised!" she said.

"What? How is that possible?" I said. I soon learned that at the last minute CBS decided to bump my race. Instead, it ran a story about Mary Slaney, the most famous and successful U.S. women's middle-distance runner ever. The International Amateur Athletic Federation had just announced her suspension because test results had shown suspiciously high testosterone levels in her system.

This was like a bad dream. We couldn't believe it. After being included in the promotional posters, all the pre-race functions and so many media stories, I felt like the Paralympic movement had been kicked in the groin. It was also humiliating for me personally, especially since the CEO of Flex-Foot, my major sponsor, invited fifty people to his home to watch my race.

The only consolation was that the CBC, the Canadian television network, did carry the race on a two-hour taped delay.

Alison declared it discrimination. "Disabled athletes didn't merit the same attention as the other athletes. CBS must have believed that disabled runners would hurt their ratings," She said.

After my singed feelings recovered a bit, I had a more benign reaction. My guess is that a single CBS producer made a poor on-the-spot decision. If he'd had time to think about and discuss it with his colleagues, he would have definitely televised my race. He simply made a hasty decision and wasn't thinking about how it might affect those of us who were excluded. I didn't think there was anything more to read into it.

Five days later, CBS did carry the race and my interview on its Friday night program, *Extra*. Of course, the viewership was a fraction of what it would have been.

Larry, too, was disappointed but unbowed. He was never short on dreams and schemes. Right away, he was talking about a rematch between Neil and me, connecting it to a possible rematch between Johnson and Bailey. Larry mused about arranging an amputee race during the halftime of a *Monday Night Football* game. His tireless efforts had met with some success. Six disabled athletes, including me, would run the 100 meters at the Goodwill Games in August. It would be the first time disabled runners would be included in the games.

Soon after the Toronto race, Coach Hoddle and I had a falling out. A runner named Marlon Shirley, who had been training with Bryan and me for some time, had been planting seeds of doubt in Bryan's head about my dedication to my track career. For example, if traffic caused me to show up five minutes late to practice after a 30 mile drive, Marlon would tell Bryan it was an example of my not being devoted to my training. Eventually Bryan and I decided, quite amicably, to go our separate ways.

Now without a coach for the first time in two years, I kept training—but soon suffered a bruised bone on the heel of my left leg. Despite the pain, Larry and I flew to Springfield, Massachusetts, for the nationals in early July. After seeing me limp through a warm-up drill, Tony Russell, a Flex-Foot rep, approached me.

"If it hurts, why are you running?" he asked.

"I feel obligated to. Flex-Foot sponsors me to run. That's what I get paid to do. That's what I'm supposed to do," I said.

Russell pointed out the obvious: It would be better to rest the injury and not risk making it worse. He was absolutely right. I withdrew from the competition.

A few weeks later, feeling better, I resumed my training. I was still fully committed to running, which meant I must put school on hold for a while longer. At least Alison was in school. When she graduated, she would be able to earn a decent living. When I aged out of competition, she would be able to support the family until I figured out a new career.

In the meantime, I still had miles to go before I slept.

Chapter 15

Becoming a Father, Regaining My Faith

In the second year of our marriage, Alison became pregnant. Even though the doctors had told us not to worry, we were concerned. They performed some tests early in the pregnancy and we were thrilled to hear that the baby had no birth defects! We later had a scare when the ultrasound picked up a lump on the baby's neck, but it turned out to be nothing.

Our beautiful and perfectly normal son, Alex, was born in May 1998. I compared my baby pictures with him. He looked exactly like me, as an infant, except he had hands and feet! When I held his tiny body in my arms, I was overwhelmed with emotion. I thought the same thing my mother did when she held me for the first time: "Now I know what my mission in life is."

As they got to know me better, Alison's parents began to realize that their daughter hadn't made such a bad decision after all, especially since I was soon able to assume the responsibility of paying for her college tuition. When she eventually graduated with a degree in chemistry, she would have no student loans to pay off.

Alison and I had had to learn how to live with and adapt to each other. For her, that meant finding out what I could and could not do. It was the little things that I had trouble with. When I was in high school, it was opening my combination lock while holding an armful of books. When I took a part-time job in a computer store after graduating high school, I wasn't able to make change for customers fast enough.

At home, I have a little trouble reaching for a glass of water across the table or turning the dial on the radio. Due to my lack of hands, my reach is ten inches shorter than it should be.

Alison knew I could butter my own roll at dinner, but if we were dressed up to go out, she would butter it for me so I wouldn't get any on my suit. Alison was always careful not to assume the role of a well-meaning nursemaid. Our policy was always "shared chores." It's not like I was helpless.

I drive a car without modifications, use utensils without alterations, and get through a day's tasks without much assistance. It may take me a little longer, but I always get the job done. A blessing of my disability is that it has allowed me to do something every self-help book ever written espouses: live in the present moment. Instead of just thoughtlessly opening a jar, for instance, I have to stop and consider it first. What is inside the jar? Is it something messy? Is the jar glass or plastic? If the jar is glass and contains something like pickles, that might slosh around if I grip it between my knees, then I need to think about what I am wearing. If I am in dress clothes and need to go to work soon, I need to be more careful or forego the pickles altogether.

Of course this all happens quickly, but I do need to go through the steps in my head. I truly believe that this focus on small things like a jar of pickles helped me as an athlete. Thought and consideration, mindfulness and concentration, is part of everything I do.

My next big competition on my way to the Sydney Paralympics took place in 1999 in Beaverton, Oregon, at the U.S. Track and Field Championships. The event promoters were able to set up a 100-meter amputee exhibition race, featuring the top three amputees in the world at the time. There were eight of us in all, but the focus was really on me, Marlon Shirley, who had trained with me for many years, and Brian Frasure. Brian had run the fastest time in the world at the time and was the favorite. Marlon had also run some incredible times that year. I was more focused on peaking for the 1999 Amputee World Championships in Barcelona, Spain, where my world records had first been set.

The process of "peaking" has six phases, each using distinct training methods to make sure an athlete is at his or her physical best for a race at the precise time. I was in the fourth phase of the process at this race, the point at which I would adjust my technical model and preparation for the main competition.

At this meet in Oregon, any of the three of us were capable of breaking the 100-meter world record.

After warm-ups and introductions to the capacity crowd it was time to race. The gun went up and in an instant we were off. I got a pretty good start but both Brian and Marlon got out of the blocks like rockets. I felt that they were too far ahead to catch but I tried to stay relaxed and run my own race. At the 50-meter mark I started my signature come from behind move, but I didn't feel that final gear kick in and before I knew it I was crossing the line in not first or second place, but third.

This was the first time since I had broken the world records that I had placed third in a race. Marlon ran 11.33 seconds, Brian 11.55 and my time was 11.66 seconds. Although Marlon's time was faster than my world record of 11.36 it wasn't recognized as such because there were not athletes from at least three countries competing.

After the race I was sitting in the changing area, putting my bag together, and I heard Marlon being interviewed by the press. He said that he felt amazing and predicted that he would be breaking the world records in both the 100-meter and 200-meter races in Barcelona in a few months. As he made this prediction he glanced over at me.

I sat up and said, "Maybe in the 100, but the 200 meters is mine! I'll be back, Marlon!"

Just after I said that I heard a voice behind me utter, "Those are the famous last words." I turned to see who would say such a thing and to my amazement it was Alison's stepfather, Jim, who had come to see her and watch me run. Although Alison's parents had never been 100 percent accepting of me, this still shocked me. I felt like he had been waiting for an opportunity to say something disapproving.

If I had been looking for motivation, I found it in this line. This proverbial slap in the face angered me and also made me determined to prove him wrong. Still, hearing words of disapproval from someone who should be one of my supporters planted a small seed of self-doubt. Was this it for me? Had my time on top come to an end?

With that, I turned my focus to the world championships in Barcelona.

The next few months were my "peaking" months as the championships drew closer. I would continue to make adjustments and then gain more competition experience. I raced in a few able-bodied all-comers events in preparation, but no more big main events.

After those couple of months passed, the time had arrived to depart once again for Spain. Returning to where it all began for me was very special. The city of Barcelona was filled with a certain energy that I thrived on. I felt that in this place I could not be beat. Still, after that race in Oregon, I struggled back and forth between self-doubt and overwhelming confidence. How would the city treat me this time? Was the magic from 1992 still here for me?

As the plane set down in Spain I felt a stirring inside me. It grew as I gathered my belongings. When I set foot on Barcelona soil I felt a rush of energy hit me. It sounds strange but the nervous butterflies in my stomach lined up and started to fly in formation, turning any negative energy into powerful positive energy. My thoughts of doubt dissolved and all I could think of was getting on the track and taking back my crown.

As the days passed and the event drew closer I tried my best to not let my competitors know how I felt. I remained as the fly on the wall and chose to just observe and listen rather than get caught up in any discussions on how I felt or how I would perform. I had a week to prepare from the time I landed until the competition took place—and those seven days felt like an eternity. I had never felt so ready for anything, so anxious to get on the track.

When race day finally arrived I sprang from my bed completely refreshed. I ate breakfast in the community hall and literally felt my legs twitching, like there was electricity trying to escape. Soon after breakfast I assembled with the other American athletes for a quick Team USA meeting and then departed for the track.

When I arrived I felt that electricity from breakfast start to swell in my legs. I knew I needed to take it easy, as I was scheduled to run four races on this tenth day of August: a semi and final in the 100 meters, and a semi and final in the 200 meters. I thought I would use my 100-meter semi as a good warm-up to the rest of the day.

Just like in Oregon a few months earlier, my main competition at these games was Marlon Shirley and Brian Frasure. Today would be different. I had pushed out all my self-doubt when the plane landed here in Spain. I felt more ready than ever. I couldn't wait to let that energy out of my legs.

To add to the build up for the main event, the 100-meter final, the event organizers broke me, Marlon and Brian out into the three separate semifinal races.

Marlon was first to go and as expected he easily won his heat and posted a time of 11.52 seconds. I was next and also won my heat with a time of 11.55 seconds. Brian was last to go and won his heat with a time of 11.60 seconds. After the race I went to the results posting board and looked at our three times. I remember thinking that I had run at about 95 percent full speed, and even though I couldn't tell at what percentage Brain or Marlon ran their heats, I knew I was right there with them.

I only had about an hour before the final so I found a free sports therapist and got a quick, light massage, and then continued to move about the track to stay warm.

As the 100-meter finals drew closer I started to ramp up my warm-ups. On my last wind sprint before we were called for the race I felt another gear kick in—one that I hadn't felt since my win in Atlanta. The electricity was trying to escape. This was a far more relaxed event than the Paralympic Games. The atmosphere was more spirited and less serious; at least that's how it felt to me. Finally the race was announced and I jogged over to the starting area.

Since Marlon, Brian and I had all won our hearts, we were lined up together in the middle of the track, as is customary. We took our warm-up starts and then it was time to settle in behind our blocks and await the starter's commands.

"Runners to your marks!" he yelled. I stared at the back of my blocks and waited for the others to get into position before stepping into my blocks. I slowly positioned my feet into the pads and rested my hands atop my foam-topped paint cans. I rocked myself from left to right and then came to a stop. "Set!" I raised myself up, coiled like I had done so many times before, waiting for the sound of the gun so I could finally let some of this energy out.

Boom!

As the gun went off we all rocketed out of the blocks. Marlon and Brian both got out quickly as usual. Unlike back in Oregon, I had a really good start myself, and trailed Marlon by only about four meters. I knew at this point that as long as I ran within myself and ran *my* race, I had enough room to catch them both. As we approached 60 meters I started my signature come from behind. I inched up to pass Brian and started to reel in Marlon. As I got closer and closer to Marlon I saw him glance over at me and just as we ran out of room at the finish line he let out an expletive I cannot repeat in this book.

The crowd went silent as the officials ran to the photo-finish booth. We all waited in suspense for the outcome. Did I have enough room to catch Marlon or was he able to hold me off just long enough? We waited for what seemed like forever. Then came the results: first place, with a time of 11.39 seconds, Tony Volpentest; second place, with a time of 11.41 seconds, Marlon Shirley; and third place, with a time of 11.52 seconds, Brian Frasure.

I had done it! My defeat in Oregon and Alison's stepfather's comment were not self-fulfilling prophecies. I had conquered my self-doubt and achieved redemption by winning the 100-meter final at the world championships!

As I walked away from the finish line Marlon came over to me and said, "Thanks a lot Tony, you have no idea how bad you just made me look in front of my sponsors."

Was he joking? I looked at him. His face contained only fury. I couldn't believe it. We had spent countless hours training together and Alison and I had him over for dinner at our house many times. Not only did he not congratulate me, he accused me of intentionally derailing his prospects for future sponsorship.

No thank you, I thought, *this is my moment!* I wasn't going to let him take *that* from me. I looked at Marlon and yelled, so anyone around us could hear me, "I WILL BE BREAKING THE 200-METER WORLD RECORD TODAY!" This record, the one that had eluded me since my last trip to Spain in 1992, was falling *today!* I felt so pumped. The energy in my legs really started to swell as I awaited my 200-meter semifinal event. I didn't have to wait long, either, before our event was called.

Same as in the 100 meters, Marlon, Brian and I were split up into three separate heats. Brian, who was stronger in this event than Marlon, went first and posted a blistering time of 23.62 seconds. This was only .55 seconds behind my world record of 23.07 seconds from the 1992 Paralympic Games.

Next it was my turn. I settled into my blocks without a care in the world. I wasn't going to wait until the finals to go after my record, I wanted it now. I felt too good to play games with the other runners. I knew there wasn't anyone in my heat who posed a threat, so I focused on my biggest competition—the clock. In this race I had been unable to beat the clock in seven years. I just couldn't put the pieces together at the right time to officially break that record. Well, today that was going to change. I had *zero* doubt about it. The record would fall!

The starter brought us to our marks, and I actually started thinking about how good it felt to break the record—but the gun hadn't even gone off yet to start the race. "Set." I rose slightly, ready to pounce. When the gun went off I shot like a rocket out of the blocks, one of my best starts ever. Then I just chewed up the corner and shot out from the curve to the straightaway as I'd been fired from a slingshot, with nobody within 30 meters of me. That wasn't good enough; I continued to accelerate down the straightaway, running through the finish line and taking almost the entire next corner to slow down before jogging back.

As I jogged back I noticed Brian Frasure, who hadn't left the finish line since his heat, bursting with excitement. I walked over to him and asked why he was so excited. He said, "You broke the world record, man, I just know you did!"

"Did you hear my time?" I asked.

"No, I don't know it for sure, but you came around that corner faster than I've even seen before. There's no way you didn't break the record."

Just then an official came over the speaker and announced: "Tony Volpentest has just broken the 200-meter world record with a time of 22.85 seconds!"

That was .22 seconds faster than my old record, and with a legal tailwind of +1.6 and a clean doping test it was now the time to beat.

After all that Marlon now had to run his heat. He also posted a fast time of 24.16 seconds, but looked like he was jogging the last 20 meters or so.

At last came the finals. I was determined to break my brand-new record. We were once again lined up in order of how we placed in our semifinals, and the race started. Although I wasn't the fastest out of the blocks I still got out very well and quickly made up the stagger on the field as we ran the corner. My philosophy in the 200 was that the first one out of the corner wins. I ran that first 100 meters like never before, coming out with about a 10-meter lead on Brian and Marlon. As we ran down the 100-meter stretch I extended the lead to about 15 meters and easily won my second world championship title of these games. Brian followed in second place and Marlon right behind in third.

We all waited for our times, and as they were announced I let out a gasp as I heard: "First place with a time of 22.87 seconds, Tony Volpentest." I had missed breaking the world record I had just established not more than two hours earlier by .02 seconds. At least I knew that my first run was no fluke; I was now a sub-23-second, 200-meter sprinter. Brian's time was 23.20 and Marlon's 23.49; both were faster than their semifinals.

When I returned to my room I called my wife to give her the news. Not wanting to gloat in front of the other athletes I played it cool, and calmly told her I had won both races and broke the world record in the 200 meters in the process. Little did I know that she took my humbleness as a sign that I was not excited about or proud of my accomplishment.

This little fact wouldn't blindside me until about a year later—which brings me to Sydney, Australia, and the 2000 Paralympic Games.

Chapter 16

Winds of Change

Athletically, 1999 had been an up-and-down year for me. I went from losing badly in Oregon to reclaiming my title and lowering my own world record in the 200-meter race in Barcelona. I went from self-doubt to feeling invincible.

Transitioning to the new millennium, I took stock of my athletic career. My glory days as an athlete were not endless; an athlete is only as good as his last race. I wouldn't be young and strong forever, and knew that one day I would have to move on to something else. Besides the glory and the adulation, I would someday lose my income from track. I needed to think about providing for my family in some other way.

Thankfully, Alison had graduated from college with honors and began working as a chemist—after staying home with Alex for the first two years of his life. The fact that I was no longer paying her tuition and that she was bringing home a paycheck helped tremendously.

But what was I going to do? I couldn't earn a living coaching Paralympic track.

This is one of the downsides that most people don't think much about when they go "gaga" over their sports heroes. First, it's tough to step out of the limelight, knowing that second high-visibility acts are extremely rare. And second, how are you going to pay the mortgage and feed your family?

As I'm sure you know, 56-game-hitting-streak New York Yankees outfielder Joe DiMaggio married Marilyn Monroe, became a sponsor for Mr. Coffee, and was the first to sell his autograph, (which is probably why he didn't give away any freebies at that banquet we attended in Las Vegas). The dream of Babe Ruth—the Bambino and the Sultan of Swat—was to manage the Yankees, but it came to naught, and his post-playing career was nothing to write home about. However, Cleveland Brown's running back Jim Brown—perhaps the greatest football player ever—went on to a very successful film career. San Francisco 49ers clutch quarterback Joe Montana did commercials for Schick razor blades, and New York Jets' quarterback Joe Namath—who predicted and won the storied Super Bowl III—did commercials for Noxzema and Beautymist pantyhose. Olympic figure-skating champion Dick Button went on to graduate from Harvard Law School and enjoyed a successful career as an actor and TV commentator.

But what about track stars? How do they fare after retirement?

Pavoo Nurmi, the Finnish middle- and long-distance Olympic champion in the 1920s, ended up running a clothing store and a small housing construction company. Sir Roger Bannister—first man to break the four-minute mile—became a distinguished neurologist and medical school professor. Jesse Owens, who won four gold medals—to the chagrin of Adolph Hitler at the 1936 Olympic Games in Berlin—struggled to make ends meet after he lost his amateur status. While white former Olympians, like Johnny Weismuller and Buster Crabbe, got film roles because of their athletic fame, this was not available to African-American Owens. After the Olympics, he raced for money against cars and horses. He was a business owner but went bankrupt. Eventually, he found his calling as a public relations consultant and motivational speaker.

These were all "mainstream" track stars. People had heard of them. But even among people who *did* follow track many, if not most, were probably unfamiliar with disabled athletes, no matter how great our success. So where did that leave me?

It had me a bit worried. The Sydney Paralympics in 2000 might be my last hurrah. My endorsements were beginning to shrink. The same companies that had been paying me for the last eight years to represent their products were now dividing that cash among more athletes. While there were more disabled athletes, which was good for the sport, the companies were eager to get more athletes involved and compensated without really being any more out of pocket. While I'm sure they increased their budgets they also started to take away from a few of us who were more highly paid, and moved toward more incentive-based deals. Corporate America wasn't yet involved in endorsement deals with Paralympians. (Fortunately, that would change in the coming decade.)

But 2000 was an Olympic year. The games were to be held in Sydney, Australia, from mid September to October 1st. The Paralympics would begin in the same venue fifteen days later. If I could win a couple of gold medals and break a world record or two, I could live off of endorsements for the next four years, deferring the inevitable for a little longer.

After Alison graduated from college in 1999, we decided to move to Chandler, Arizona, along with my brother Mike and his wife Tana. We were all tired of the rain and gloomy skies of the Pacific Northwest. I had always trained in the cool damp climate of Seattle but had competed in warmer regions and did well in the heat. I figured if I trained in and got acclimated to a warmer place, maybe it would help me reach the next level athletically.

I quickly discovered that training in the 110 degree heat and sunshine of Arizona was no picnic. While doing wind sprints on a nearby track one day, I passed out. Fortunately, some workmen preparing the outdoor stadium for a high-school graduation that weekend discovered me. I woke up to a groundskeeper standing over me, spraying me with a hose to cool me down.

I also started to notice a few subtle changes in my marriage. Alison seemed more distant and less affectionate. Was it my imagination? Was I being too sensitive? After all, she had landed her first post-graduate job as a chemist. It was probably very stressful. She would come home tired and irritable. Maybe that was the extent of it. Or maybe it was my training. While she supported that part of my life, she also wanted me to be working, as I wasn't making as much money on the track anymore. Every marriage has its ups and downs. But still, I couldn't help but worry. Uncertain about how I would fare financially after the 2000 Paralympics, I decided to explore a career in information technology. I landed an entry-level job in the IT division of a large stock-brokerage firm. I was not an employee, but a contractor with no benefits. I got a 1099 statement of income earned at the end of the year, but it was additional income the family needed.

In the meantime, I continued to train full time. This year, however, I was training on my own. I'd had no coach since Bryan and I went our separate ways. I simply couldn't afford one.

It is one thing to train while working full time, but training while working full time without a coach is a hardship. There are days when I lacked the will to drag myself out to the track because I was so exhausted, but when I looked into the eyes of my little boy, I became reenergized.

Day after day, I slipped out of bed at 4 A.M. to go to work. The firm I worked for had to support the opening of the financial markets—which is 9:30 A.M. Eastern Time, and we were in Arizona, in the Pacific Time Zone most of the year. And after work, I'd hit the track. My wife and I were working so hard—not to mention juggling child care—we more or less waved to one another as we went past.

To keep sharp, I entered several local able-bodied events, but something was missing. In July, I competed in the 2000 U.S. Track and Field Olympic Team Trials in Sacramento, California, and turned in one of my slowest 100-meter times—12.88 seconds—since I started running on the Flex-Foot. I seemed incapable of shifting into that final turbo-charged gear I had become famous for. Like virtually all human endeavors, including sports, one's mental state is critical. I needed to re-charge my psyche.

The morning before my next able-bodied race in Tucson, Alison and I decided to take our son to Sedona for the day. When we arrived and drove around, I was surprised that this magical place—famous for its stunning and unique sandstone rock formations, which glow in dazzling oranges and reds when the sun is rising or setting—hadn't been declared a national park. It has many winding miles of biking and hiking trails, but it is also a magnet for those in pursuit of spiritual reawakening.

Not surprisingly, a specialized New Age tourist industry had sprung up in Sedona around the notion of "harmonic convergences", also known as "spiritual vortices." These are supposed pockets of energy that people feel, from which they draw inspiration and renewal. According to those in the know, such pockets are concentrated at Bell Rock, Airport Mesa, Cathedral Rock, and Boynton Canyon.

Since I was suffering from a spiritual crisis in my marriage and on the track, I found myself drawn to some kind of paranormal treatment.

We decided to take a hike up to the Bell Rock Vortex. While resting on the way down, I started to notice my energy level rising. Maybe I was just vulnerable to the power of suggestion. Next, we drove up to the Airport Mesa Vortex. Once we got there, something felt different. At the top of the mesa, I felt a rush of energy. Feeling a little light headed, I sat down next to the edge of an escarpment across from Bell Rock. After a time, my entire body started to vibrate. Alison walked over with Alex in her arms and put her right hand on my left knee to balance herself.

Looking a bit shocked, she said, "Tony, you're trembling."

I was relieved to know that I was not hallucinating.

When I woke up the next morning back home, I felt transfixed. I was alive with confidence and energy. Once again, I felt invincible. I packed my bags and departed for my race in Tucson.

Worried that I would be stiff after the nearly three-hour drive there, I took extra time warming up. Today, I would only be running the 200 meters, because the 100- and 200-meter competitions are alternated every week. Usually by this time of the year, I should be running in the mid to high 23's. In my most recent race, I ran a relatively slow 24.3 seconds. Today, I really needed to burn rubber and take it under 24, so I could arrive in Sydney believing I had a realistic shot at another—and probably my final—Paralympic gold medal.

As the time for my 200-meter race drew closer, I started to feel really loose. I hadn't felt this relaxed in a long time.

Finally, my race was called. In this able-bodied event, I would be lining up against several high-school varsity athletes, a few walk-ons like me, as well as a couple of college sprinters. As I settled into my blocks, I felt a peaceful calm surge over me. As the starter raised the gun, I felt an electrical charge rush through my legs. The gun went off. I blasted out of the blocks.

Coming around the corner, I felt like my old self as I hit the straightaway. The missing gear that had eluded me all season was back. I was the first one across the finish line with a time of 22.8! I had run under my official world record time from the World

Championships in Barcelona last year. Pity it didn't count as a world record.

With renewed confidence, I was ready for Sydney.

About a month before the games, I decided to approach Ross Perot again. I asked him if he would consider paying for Alison and Alex to come to Australia with me. Alison and I had spoken about her coming, but had dismissed the idea because we couldn't afford it. She would be thrilled to visit Down Under. Who wouldn't be?

I called Perot from work. He said he would be delighted to pay their expenses. In a matter of hours, his assistant had made all the arrangements. I would be staying in the athletes' village and Alison and Alex would be staying in a fancy hotel downtown next to the famous Sydney Opera House, one of the iconic buildings of the twentieth century. I was excited for all of us.

When I called to give her the good news, there was a long pause.

"I'm not sure I'll be able to get the time off," she said.

I laughed. She couldn't be serious. "Well, just go ask your boss," I said.

She pushed back again: "I don't think I'm going to be able to get the time off."

I told her to explain that her husband was competing in Sydney, Australia, in the equivalent of the Olympics for amputees. Of course he would give her the time off.

"No, I won't be able to get the time off. We're extremely busy," she said stubbornly.

"You won't even ask?" I said.

"No, I don't think it's a good idea."

That's when I really started to worry.

Still, I wanted to believe her. She couldn't really talk about what she did at work. I think her company supplied chemicals to Intel and NASA, including the fuel for the Space Shuttle. Maybe she was afraid it wouldn't look good if she asked for some time off. There had been rumors of a layoff, so maybe she felt she couldn't give her supervisors any reason to give her a pink slip.

Whatever the reason, there was no chance she would change her mind.

As October rolled around, Alison grew more distant. She stayed late at the office more often. I asked her all the normal things you might say in a situation like this. "Have I done something?"

"No, you've been great," she would say. She said she was unhappy. She seemed unable to say why. And when she tried, her explanations were vague. She'd go for walks with my sister-in-law, Tana, but she couldn't get any information out of Alison either.

Of course, this affected my training. I was worried and distracted. I couldn't help but feel less motivated, because my home life was no longer happy and stable. The future seemed uncertain and foreboding.

I planned to arrive in Sydney at least two weeks early. The general rule is that for every hour spent in the air, it takes a day to recover one's peak performance. Therefore, with a fifteen-hour flight, I needed to get there at least two weeks before my first race.

Finally, on October 1, we drove to the airport. My heart was heavy. Most athletes thrive on support, especially at big events. My parents were making the trip from Seattle, but my wife and son would be missing in action. Alison hugged me goodbye and wished me good luck, but it seemed perfunctory.

This was the worst possible prelude to an event in which every particle of one's physical and spiritual being must be positively energized in absolute harmony in order to have any shot at beating the best in the world.

The flight was interminable. I couldn't sleep. I walked up and down the aisle. I couldn't stop thinking about Alison and questioning myself. We had been married six years. What had I done wrong? What could I have done differently? Was I unhappy in my marriage? No, definitely not. I would do anything to save it. What's more, I think divorce has a horrible psychological effect on kids of any age, especially young kids.

I would work hard to save this marriage from whatever was happening. All I could do was try.

Chapter 17

Feeling Under, Down Under

In Sydney I went through all the usual procedures for athletes. We were processed, given credentials, and assigned to our rooms and roommates. While the athletes' rooms are never spacious, the dorms in the Paralympic Village turned out to be a bit cramped—more so than in Barcelona—and the walls paper thin. I spoke with one of the U.S. coordinators, who kindly arranged for my roommate, Jeremy Burleson, and me to be moved to a more comfortable "portable" room nearby. This was a far cry from my suite at the Marriott for the Atlanta Paralympics four years ago. Otherwise, the facilities were top notch and the officials and volunteers very helpful and cordial. Unfortunately, my overall experience was overshadowed by the uncertainty of what was happening back home.

Jeremy was a muscular, blond Southerner, and stood nearly six feet tall. A single below the knee amputee, he was competing in the grueling pentathlon, which consisted of: running the 100 meters and 400 meters; doing the long jump and the shot put; and hurling the discus. (He would eventually place fourth in the pentathlon, missing the bronze by a whisker.)

There's an unspoken brotherhood with the athletes you share your living space with and Jeremy and I bonded right away, like he was one of my own brothers. My parents also took to him and referred to him as one of their own. He had a dry, quick-witted personality, was easygoing and always willing to listen. Thus, I confided in him about my marital troubles. He listened, though he wasn't presumptuous enough to give advice, and made me laugh when he saw me about to plunge into a black-hole mood.

For most athletes, the opening ceremonies are one of the highlights of the Olympic or Paralympic experience. Marching as a team into the stadium behind the stars and stripes is something you never forget. However, I chose not to march in with the team. Instead, I sat in the stands with my parents. I decided that since my first race was only a few days away, it would be best to save myself from the long wait in line before marching in. The truth is I was not feeling the spirit of these games. Jeremy decided to join me and my family in the stands because he was feeling homesick.

Finally, it was October 20; the day of my 100-meter semifinal race.

I woke up feeling under the weather. I visited the U.S. medical team and they concluded that I was dehydrated. They told me to drink a lot of water. My event wasn't scheduled until 5:00 P.M., so I went back to bed knowing I had many hours to relax and rehydrate. An hour later, I had my usual egg and toast breakfast. Gloomily, I sat in the dining hall for a few hours, drinking juice, watching athletes come and go, and staring into space.

Finally, Jeremy found me and sat down. Again, we grappled with my issues back home, which we both knew were going to interfere with my performance. While there was no way I could pretend this wasn't happening; I needed to banish the worry from my head for a little while. Allowing this to rob me of a chance at Paralympic gold made no sense, especially since nothing I did or thought here would make any difference back in Arizona.

I arrived at the warm-up track about two hours before my event. Going through the motions of my normal warm-ups, I definitely didn't feel as good as I had prior to my races so far that year. My body seemed slow and sluggish. Try as I might to block out my emotional distractions; they just kept creeping back in, leaving me depressed and anxious.

Brian Fraser and Neil Fuller were running in the first heat. I was in the second; Marlon Shirley in the third. We all warmed up together. Everyone else seemed to be in top form, seemingly without a care in the world, relaxed and not bothered or distracted. I, however, couldn't seem to summon the inner will to drive away my troubles.

First call for my event was announced. I gathered my things and lethargically walked over to the first check-in point. After that, sitting next to my bag, I waited in a quiet area away from the others. Normally I would be dancing and moving around to make sure my body didn't cool down. This time I was indifferent. I so wanted and needed to get back in the zone, but I just couldn't seem to light that fire.

The second and third calls came and went. Standing in the tunnel, about to enter the stadium, I felt blessed to be in my third Paralympics. I hoped it wouldn't be my last and I really wanted to make a good showing. But instead of feeling pumped and excited, I felt listless. Some of the usual energy sparked, however, as we entered the venue and stepped onto the track.

As we walked around the outer ring of the stadium in single file, I watched the first semifinal heat. As expected, Fraser won easily with a time of 11.53 seconds. Fuller came in second with 11.86.

I was up next. Shirley was waiting in the wings for the third heat.

My semifinal was announced and I started arranging my blocks.

The only sprinter in my heat who was a possible threat was Marcus Ehm from Germany. He has been consistently improving year after year, and I wasn't sure what his fastest time was that year. No matter, I just had to run my best race and get to the finals.

The starter called us to our blocks. One final time, I struggled to clear my mind of all irrelevant debris. As I settled, I thought of my son Alex. No matter what happened, he would always be paramount in my life. Being a father had rewards far beyond racing and gold medals. That thought calmed and settled me.

The starter continued: "Set." I rose up, suddenly feeling like a loose spring rather than a tight one.

Boom!

I popped out of the blocks and immediately stood straight up instead of staying in my usual lower-drive position. Thankfully, my muscle memory took over and I finished strong, winning my heat in 11.83, slightly faster than Fuller's semifinal time. Ehm was right behind me in 12.10. At the very least, I should win the bronze.

This was one of my slowest times of the year, but I tried to stress the positive. I was still in contention, and at least I had secured a spot in the next day's finals. I would have my work cut out for me, however. In the third heat, Shirley ran a blistering 11.31 and broke my world record.

Afterward, I joined my family in the stands. They congratulated me, telling me I ran a great race. They were convinced that I performed the way I did to conceal from my rivals what I was really capable of. I didn't let on that I was really just distracted and not right in the head. They had no idea what was going on in my private life. Why upset them over something that may turn out to be a minor hiccup?

I returned to the village for dinner and rest. Then I started to feel ill. Maybe I was still feeling the effects of dehydration, plus I was a ball of stress. I called home to talk to Alison and Alex. "Hey,

I won my heat and qualified for the finals!" I said, trying to be as cheerful as possible. I hoped to hear some words of encouragement from my wife. Instead, there was an awkward silence, then words that felt like a kick in the gut.

"Tony, I think I want a divorce."

I was speechless. I began to hyperventilate. Finally, I managed to squeeze out a few words. I haltingly told her, "I need to go and rest, please give Alex a kiss for me and tell him I love him."

After hanging up, I thought, Here I am, on the far side of the world. It's the 2000 Paralympic Games—the night before my 100-meter final. Couldn't she have waited a few days to tell me such crushing news?

Later she would tell me that the same thought occurred to her—immediately after she had blurted out her feelings.

After that nightmarish conversation, things went from bad to worse. I started feeling feverish. I skipped dinner and headed to the infirmary. Checking the thermometer, the nurse said, "You have a temperature of 103, and you are dehydrated." The medical staff considered starting me on an IV drip but decided to keep me for observation. They had me suck on ice and drink fluids. A few hours later, I returned to my room. I lay awake all night, staring at the cracks in the ceiling.

My fever never abated and that, coupled with my emotional turmoil, made for a sleepless night. I dragged myself out of bed the next morning. It took a few hours to get ready. If I was to perform today, I needed to keep hydrated and force down some food. Jeremy and I walked to the dining hall and sat at our usual table. "Man, you look like crap," he said, shaking his head. I told him about my conversation with Alison. He couldn't believe she would be so thoughtless the night before my final.

Trying to get my mind off of Alison, he pointed out all the

beautiful women walking by. All athletes, they were all fit, of course. One of the Swedish team members walked by and gave us a big smile. "See," he said, "they are all around here and I've seen more than a few checking you out."

While he had good intentions, I hadn't noticed and really didn't care about any of these other women. I still loved my wife, I was still a married man and I honored my vows—despite what was facing me when I returned home. I returned to my room, packed up my gear, and headed out to the stadium.

On the way, I almost fell asleep. I was physically and emotionally spent. After arriving at the warm-up track, I came across a couple of prosthetists, who were stationed on the track to assist anyone who needed help. They asked if everything felt okay with my legs. I explained that my Flex-Feet seemed a little stiff. They had a couple that were slightly less stiff and offered to substitute them right there on the track. This was equivalent to a NASCAR driver saying his tires were too slick and having his pit crew replace them. Although last-minute substitutions are not uncommon at these events, I had always opted not to make changes the day of a race, never mind minutes before it. Today, however, was not like any other day. I allowed them to make the switch.

Swapping out my feet ate into my warm-up time. Before I knew it, first call was announced. I barely had time to try running on my new feet before I was passing the first check-in point. After getting settled into the second staging area, I started vigorously warming up. Now, too late, I noticed that one of my legs was a bit too short. I felt like I was running with a slight limp. I called the men back over. After measuring the length difference, one of the prosthetists determined that there was in fact a one-inch difference between my left and right legs. He offered to quickly switch the feet back to my originals, just as third call was announced. I was standing at the final check-in point and you only have five minutes between calls. I didn't want to risk it because if I didn't move along, I would be disqualified. I had no choice but to stick with what I had.

I entered the last staging area and tried to do a few more wind sprints. But I found myself in the middle of the perfect storm. I had been up all night with a fever, reeling over Alison's pronouncement, and then I had stupidly allowed my legs—with which I've always been happy—to be tampered with. To top it off I felt stiff and cold. I was in no condition to race, never mind win a medal or break a world record.

But none of that mattered now. My 100-meter final had just been called. I was ushered into the stadium—along with Frasure, Shirley, Fuller, and my other rivals—for what had been billed as one of the premier events at these games. All week the American press had been predicting the United States would easily sweep this event because we had the three fastest qualifiers, including myself, in the previous day's semifinals.

Based on these reports, the sweep should have been a shoo-in. I knew it wouldn't be and that I needed a miracle to pull out a win here.

The jolt of electricity I had always felt as I made my way onto the track was not there, not even a spark. I conjured up an image of my son for inspiration. But that turned into more questions and worry: what would life be like as a single dad when I returned home? What would Alex's life be like with a broken home? He was only two years old and soon wouldn't even remember us living together as a family.

As each athlete was introduced and his photo displayed on the JumboTron, the crowd reacted. Naturally, Neil Fuller got the most sustained applause. He was the only Aussie in the finals and one of the most recognized Paralympians in this country.

With the introductions over, we all got in a few practice starts.

Then came time to race. Since Shirley had broken the world record in his semifinal heat, he was the clear favorite. I needed to summon enough fire power to hold off Fuller and complete the U. S. sweep.

After we were called to our marks, I stood behind them, staring off in a trance. Finally, I snapped out of it and settled into my blocks with my paint cans in front of me.

I heard the "Set" command. We rose up, and awaited the sound of the gun. *"Boom!"*

Because I wasn't focused, my reaction to it was dull, almost like I had heard it later than everyone else. Shirley shot out of his blocks like a bullet. Fraser was right behind him, followed by Fuller. My *modus operandi* was to come from behind, so I did not panic. As we all flew down the track, I tried to activate my high gear so I could overtake Fuller and possibly Fraser. Shirley was too far ahead to catch in the few seconds remaining. Each time I tried to kick into my high gear, I felt like I was going to fall. I realized that the "one-inch blunder" was going to cost me the bronze and deny us an American sweep.

In the blink of an eye, we crossed the finish line. Moments later, we learned that Shirley had again broken the world record with a blistering time of 11.09 seconds. Fraser took the silver with 11.46, and Fuller the bronze with 11.65. I came in fourth with 11.81—slightly better than my semifinal heat, but not good enough.

After the race, I congratulated Shirley and then quickly retreated, desperately searching for an exit. I wanted to put this race behind me, knowing that at least I still had my favorite event—the 200 meters—to look forward to. But before I could vanish, several reporters surrounded me. It cost me nothing to be magnanimous, so instead of making excuses for myself I focused on my rivals' performances. I gave credit where credit was due.

When asked about my performance, I just shrugged. Of course, I was very disappointed. I didn't run my best race. It happens—you just hope it doesn't happen in the Paralympics.

I joined my family outside the stadium. As usual, my parents were supportive. They sensed that something was weighing me down, but they didn't pry, and I didn't want to say anything to them until I'd spoken to Alison again, but I could call her only from the Village. Regardless, I was so grateful they were there; their presence gave me a shoulder to lean on. They understood how much pressure I was under. My endorsements depended on how well I performed. Most of my sponsors paid me a small monthly stipend, but each of them gave me a $5,000 bonus for a world record or gold medal. These bonuses add up quickly, as they did when I won in Barcelona and Atlanta.

Nonetheless, all was not lost. My 200-meter semifinal heat was two days away. It had become my favorite race, because I had an extra 100 meters to make up for my inherently slow starts.

As the idle days between my two races passed by, I started to relax. My confidence started to rebound. My fever had subsided and I felt much better. I knew that on any given race day, anything was possible. I still had hope—and that was a good thing.

I felt pretty good on the morning of my semifinal. I had a relaxing morning in the village, ate my light breakfast at my leisure, and then departed for the stadium. I had gone back to my original feet, and I arrived at the track with plenty of time to warm up. I had not run once since my 100-meter loss, because I wanted to conserve everything for this race. I did a few wind sprints to confirm that my prostheses were feeling perfect.

After a round of skipping drills and stretching, I did a series of progressively faster wind sprints. I had time left to get a quick massage. I waited until I got through the second checkpoint before I put on both of my feet and resumed my warm-ups. I felt great. I was going to run a really fast race. This time I would find that extra gear, I just knew it.

The final call came. I entered the last staging area with the other competitors. A few moments later, we gathered our things and lined up before entering the stadium.

As I walked in, serenity enveloped me. For years, sports psychologists had taught me how to convert negative energy and nervousness into rocket fuel. I had a programmed word—in my case, "snow"—that took me to my quiet, serene place. I was somehow able to draw from my crisis back home, as well as my dismal performance in the 100-meter final, and channel it into a powerful confidence.

We made our way around the stadium to the 200-meter start. I took a few moments to set up my paint cans and adjust my blocks. I then ran a few practice starts. Again, each athlete was introduced on the JumboTron. I was smiling. This was going to be my best race ever. I hadn't felt so good, so confident, or so certain since I arrived in Sydney.

Finally, we were called to our blocks.

I took my time, making sure that my "feet" were lined up precisely. As I settled into the pre-set race position, I felt completely at peace. Today, I was the world's fastest greyhound. I would literally roar around the first turn.

The starter shouted, "Set!" I rose up, coiled, ready.

The gun went off. I hurtled out of the blocks, feeling the clawing and tearing of my spikes on the track. My push phase was flawless as I rapidly transitioned into my acceleration phase. It seemed as if I was on a treadmill, as though the track was effortlessly flying by under my feet. I was not even sure my feet were touching the ground. As I hit the 60-meter mark coming around the turn, I knew my high gear was about to kick in. But I was shocked. I didn't feel my usual turbo-charged gear. Instead, I felt something I had never before experienced. I accelerated faster and faster around the corner. I was *flying!*

As I was about to transition into the straightaway, I realized I was going too fast. The centrifugal force was pulling me out of my lane. I fought to stay in it, as I prepared to slingshot myself out into the straightaway. And then it happened. My right hamstring tore away from the femur. The pain was searing, as though someone had impaled me with a red-hot knife. My own body took me down, as I fell hard, shoulder first, onto the track. Instinctively, I tumbled and twisted out of the away to avoid the other runners. When I came to a full stop, I was totally disoriented. As I sprawled on the track, writhing in pain, time came to a complete stop. Sound was muffled. I winced from the excruciating pain but then stopped when I opened my eyes and saw the Paralympic flame. I gazed at it for what felt like hours. How different these games were from Barcelona and Atlanta. Would this injury prevent me from ever seeing another Paralympic flame?

Finally, the officials and trainers scraped me off the track. They put me in a wheelchair and immediately took me to the medical staff.

While I was being examined, one of the U.S. coaches told me that he had clocked my first 100 meters at 10.8 seconds—faster than I had ever run before, and faster than Marlon's world record time. I was thrilled to hear that. Honestly, a few days earlier I thought that my best days were behind me and that maybe my mojo was gone for good. Despite my injury, this news made me want to keep fighting. The Paralympics in Athens were only four years away.

But with the Sydney games now in the books, I first had to face a long flight back home—and an uncertain future.

Chapter 18

My True North

I tried to put the pieces of my marriage back together. I suggested seeing a marriage counselor. Alison agreed to go and got a recommendation from a co-worker, a man. As I found out later, however, they had been seeing each other outside the office.

Alison and I went to one session together, then I went to two sessions alone, and then she went to half of one session before returning home to announce that the counselor didn't know what she was doing. I went back to see the counselor one last time to see what had happened. She said that when she started to tell Alison the things she needed to work on, Alison got up and left saying, "You don't know what you're talking about."

Reaching this impasse, divorce was inevitable. I accepted this outcome with as much grace and dignity as I could muster, even though I was dying inside. I was also lonely and scared.

My parents were supportive as always. My mom counseled, "One door shuts but another one opens. You'll survive this!"

Knowing that I could not change my situation, I focused on what I could change—my reaction. I did what I had always done. I stressed the positive. While the last year of my marriage was not good, the other five years with Alison had been wonderful, and we had produced a beautiful son. Alex was the most important person in my life. Neither I, nor Alison, wanted to make this situation any harder on him than it needed to be. As much as she had hurt me, I would not be hostile toward her nor offer any recriminations. We agreed we would behave respectfully toward one another, like adults should. Hence, the divorce proceeded amicably. We saved money by using a paralegal instead of an attorney. We quickly agreed to most of the terms, including joint custody.

I would keep the four-bedroom, 2,400-square-foot Spanish-style house for the sake of Alex's sense of continuity. Alison told me that I deserved to keep it because I had worked so hard for it over the years.

Because she and I knew that we would be in constant close touch for years to come, we made a solemn pact to never put Alex in the middle of any disagreements we might have. We would be cordial and courteous to one another. Alex came first.

The divorce was finalized early in 2001. I found myself in a completely different place than I had been in a year earlier. I never could have predicted this. Out of the blue, life hands us changes and challenges us to forge ahead.

Although I pledged to keep training for the 2004 Paralympics in Athens, my endorsements had all but dried up. I had to find a way to pay the mortgage and feed my son.

In the year before Sydney, I had landed that job in the financial-services industry as a temporary contractor, but the hi-tech bubble had just burst and I was unemployed.

Because I had put higher education on hold for athletics, I didn't have a college degree. I considered coaching track, but it didn't pay what I needed. I was a good motivational speaker, but giving an occasional speech wasn't going to cover my expenses. I was going through my savings and really started to worry.

I'd always had an interest in electronics. A high-end audio/

video store was looking for a salesman. I applied for the job. Although I had no experience in sales, I did have an impressive list of accomplishments, along with an unusual personal reference on my resume—Ross Perot. When I called him and asked him if it was okay to use him, he quickly agreed.

At the end of my interview with the store manager, he looked over my resume and asked, "Is this really Ross Perot's private phone number?"

"It is," I answered.

"If I call this number and actually speak to Ross Perot, I'll hire you on the spot," he said.

Moments later I was offered the job.

While I didn't know much about sales, having people stare at me all the time had thickened my skin, making it easier for me to handle rejection—which is exactly what you need to succeed in that line of work. And I was naturally friendly and outgoing. People often buy from someone they like. This job had no salary—it was straight commission. I'd eat what I killed, so to speak. If I made the sale, that was all that would matter. It didn't have to be pretty; I had bills to pay!

I noticed that when some people came into the store, they would look down and walk away when I approached them. To put them at ease, I'd often make a joke, accompanied by a friendly smile.

"Can I give you a hand? No pun intended!" I'd say.

More times than not, the person chuckled and seemed to relax. Although I was not the highest paid salesman in the store, I was able to slow down the burn rate on my savings.

I worked there for about a year. Finally, the same financial-services company I used to work for contacted me. They had an eighteen-month project that they needed my help on. The pay was excellent. Slowly I replenished my savings.

In December of 2002, I was driving home from work, minding my own business, listening to "Eye of the Tiger" on the radio, the song from the film *Rocky*, sung by the group Survivor. Out of the blue, a car crashed into my SUV, sending me spinning and flipping over into the median strip between the freeway's north-and southbound lanes. Fortunately, I landed on all four wheels, and I didn't hit any other cars. I was wearing my seatbelt so I stayed in the vehicle, but for some reason the airbags didn't deploy.

As I sat there in a daze, completely numb, I started spitting out a few tiny shards of safety glass. All the windows were broken. I could hear air hissing from my tires. I somehow had the presence of mind to turn off the ignition before my SUV caught fire. Since I don't have fingers and I was shaking so hard, I had trouble getting out of my seatbelt. Luckily the fire department arrived quickly and helped free me from the vehicle.

The driver who caused the accident stopped and actually followed the ambulance to the hospital to check on me. He was young, so he only had the minimum $15,000 insurance coverage. I had to basically sue my own insurance company to collect on the underinsured driver coverage I had on my policy.

As frightening as this was, I counted my blessings. It could have been much worse. I had a few cuts and bruises, along with cervical whiplash. It took a couple of years of rehab until the lower-back pain finally went away. Alex was very young and a ball of energy, but he knew enough to be very patient with me.

The worst news: needless to say, there would be no comeback at the 2004 Paralympic Games in Athens. My competing days were over.

Several months after the accident my consulting contract ended again, and fortunately, I was welcomed back at the high-end audio/video store. But once again I was draining my savings. I was struggling and worried.

I needed to get back into the financial-services industry as a full-time employee. Fortunately, my brother Mike heard of an opening in just the kind of firm I wanted to work for. And after several interviews, I got the job.

Basically, my team and I made sure that the various computer and communications systems used by our traders and staff were always up and running. Most importantly, our job was to anticipate and prevent problems from ever happening.

Still, something vital was missing. I needed to find my "true north."

Of course, my most important true north I already possessed—my son Alex. He was such a sweet boy, mature beyond his years. He hardly ever misbehaved or acted out. He knew I was different from other dads, and that some tasks were more difficult for me than others, but he never complained. For example, it would take me a little longer than most parents to put on his shoes in the morning. And he knew that buttons were something I didn't particularly relish. Even at any early age, he was patient with me.

He was also tolerant with me in the kitchen, where I particularly struggle sometimes. For example, I have trouble opening bottles and jars. I'm also not very handy with a knife, so cleaning a chicken is out of the question.

This led to trouble cooking. We often ate out. When we stayed home, for ease and convenience, I often relied on packaged foods rather than making a meal from scratch. I knew plenty of able-bodied busy parents who did the same thing, of course. While what I made maybe could have been healthier, it wasn't like we were eating fast food every night. We ate together and discussed what had happened during the day. Whatever I made, I prepared with love, and I hoped that Alex knew that. I did the best I could.

Alex and I navigated the waters of a single dad-hood together. Along with being a very understanding and kind boy, he was also intelligent and well-rounded. He grew into a fine young man and was enrolled in a middle school gifted program, became an accomplished drummer, and earned a red belt in Tae Kwon Do. Watching him change before my eyes, I couldn't be prouder of him.

After my divorce, I dated casually. I was in no hurry to jump back into a serious, long-term relationship. I tried the usual venues for meeting women—bookstores, sports bars, friends, and online dating, but I had little success.

Not unsurprisingly, my physical appearance seemed to be the biggest hurdle.

After eight years, I decided it was time to take a break from my quest for someone special, so I decided to not renew my online dating membership. It had been a waste of money and time.

On the night my membership was to lapse, I took one last look just for the heck of it. I saw a new profile that really caught my eye. Forgetting that my membership was about to expire, I clicked on "wink," to indicate an interest in her. I didn't get my hopes up as I shut down the computer.

The next day, I got an email notification from the dating service that I had received a message from someone—either some girl had "winked" me, or I had been "winked" back.

I had to renew my membership just to read the message. I felt utterly foolish as I pressed the "agree to terms" button; nonetheless, I went ahead with it.

To my surprise and delight, the note was from the woman I had "winked." Her name was Kami.

She wrote that she wanted to be honest. She said that she didn't know how she might react to dating someone with a disability until she met me in person because she had never been in that kind of situation before.

I replied with this:

Good morning Kami,

Thank you very much for your email. I wasn't offended at all by what you said:) I'm not that sensitive about my "disability". I also appreciate that you don't view it as such. I don't either which is why I put it in quotes. I've been given the opportunity to see some amazing places and meet amazing people because of it.

I think it's cute that you're shy . . . I am too:) It would be my pleasure to get to know you! Your profile was such a breath of fresh air. I know what you mean about lighting the fire, as mine has been out for years too. Your description of having a strong but gentle temperament and a good heart is how I would describe myself as well. I've also always been the diplomat in my family which I would say fits the role as peacemaker:)

I could go on about the similarities I see, but like you said getting to know me is the only way one can find out. Oh, but I will throw in that I am the type of guy that has no problem showing my softer side:)

I very much look forward to learning more!

Tony

P.S. I know we're both shy and I never do this but here's my number if you'd like to chat on the phone . . .

That evening, the phone rang. It was Kami! We talked for hours. We spoke about all sorts of regular things that people getting to know each other talk about, like what do you do for a living, etc. She was very soft spoken and had a really calming demeanor. I think we were both attracted to how refreshingly honest and "real" we both were with each other. It was never a struggle to keep the conversation going. It also felt like we had already known each other our whole lives, like friends who were catching up. We also were both very much on the same intellectual level, so our talks were never forced or stalled; we both just knew what the other was saying.

The following night, we talked for hours again. We decided to take the plunge. We agreed to meet in person the following afternoon.

The next day, as I sat at a table in front of a Barnes and Noble bookstore, I watched several women walk toward the building. I knew what she was supposed to look like, but it was not unusual for there to be a discrepancy between the online photo and the real person. Then I saw her from a distance, walking across the sunny parking lot. Her long and luminous brown hair, which fell to the middle of her back, was blowing in the breeze. She was of average height—and way-above- average looks. She was stunning, far more beautiful than her online photo. My heart caught in my throat as she headed my way.

We introduced ourselves and she sat down. We were both a little nervous, but that didn't stop the flow of conversation.

She had been married for twelve years and divorced for three. She showed me photos of her three beautiful children—two daughters and a son. I took out a picture of Alex.

She told me she had Googled me and now asked me about my track days. I could tell she was still very nervous. Since we were about to talk about track, I decided to tell her about a trick my coach used to employ to make me a more relaxed sprinter. I also know that in order to demonstrate this trick, I would have to risk holding her hand. My coach had told me how he would have his athlete hold a Popsicle stick between his or her thumb and index finger, long-ways. The object of the exercise was to run without breaking the stick, thus forcing the athlete to relax. "Here, let me show you," I said, as I took a fork from the table and asked her to place it between her fingers.

I then told her about the pioneering operation I had when I was ten months old that separated the forearm bones to give me two "fingers" on each arm, and used the *pronator teres* muscles to give me a pincer-like grasp. I told her that even though I could look more "normal", my parents had elected for me not to be fitted with myoelectric hands, because they lacked all sense of touch.

She touched and examined my arms more closely. And after that, she seemed to relax.

We kept talking for over an hour. Neither of us wanted this moment to end. We decided to go for a walk in the mall.

After an hour of talking and aimless window shopping, we decided to have dinner. At the restaurant, the first thing we did was order tea. When it arrived, she asked if I'd like some sugar in it. "Two packets," I said. She opened two small sugar packets and poured them into my cup. That simple act—done without hesitation or awkwardness—spoke volumes about this woman.

After dinner, we sat on a bench, talking and gazing at a nearby water fountain. We were all alone, even though scores of shoppers were passing by.

When a guard walked up to announce that the mall would be closing in a few minutes, we were stunned. It was 10 P.M. Our first date has lasted nearly nine hours! I wanted so badly to believe that my true north has arrived.

And, indeed, it had.

We married two years later on October 16, 2010.

Not only were we married, but we also joined together our two families. Kami's children –Karlee, John and Kathryn—loved me from day one and got along great with Alex. Most of Kami's family lived in Arizona and were extremely accepting. She also came from a large family, with three brothers and two sisters. All but two are married, with children, so holidays are a blast when we all get together; we have a crowd of around thirty-five people. Kami's siblings and spouses are also very supportive and encouraging.

My family loves Kami as if she were always a part of it. My parents call three to four times a week and talk to either myself or to her alone. If it's just to me they always ask how she is and make sure I'm taking good care of her.

When my old coach, Bryan Hoddle, first met Kami he said that if I ever decided to compete again, she would be my secret weapon. Kami never fails to amaze me. She was a stay-at-home mom for twelve years, then went back to school and managed to keep a 4.0 grade-point average. After her divorce she got a job to make ends meet, starting out just above minimum wage, but then moved into the financial-services industry and has been promoted five times since we met.

We bring out the best in each other. While we don't push each other, we've each said that nothing can stop us as long as we have each other. We gain strength from one another and this propels us to strive to be better at everything we do.

My life had gone from disaster and disappointment to one of contentment and love. You never know why life leads you down a road with twists and turns and seemingly insurmountable obstacles. If I did not tear my hamstring, or get into that horrible accident, I would have kept training and traveling and I wouldn't have had time for online dating. I would never have slowed down enough to meet Kami. Mom was so right: one door closed, but another one, leading to a wonderful new life, opened when I met Kami.

Gone are the days of Alex and I eating prepackaged frozen meals. Kami prepares amazing and healthful meals for our family. I found my soul mate in Kami, loving her more than life itself. Our blended family of six is filled with diverse personalities but we all have one thing in common—love for one another. Our home is filled with happiness and laughter. Together, we are one.

Chapter 19

Full Circle: Helping Others Live Determined

"Excuse me, excuse me . . . sir? Sir!" The woman shouted as she pushed her way through the crowd. "Excuse me, please . . ." I felt a tap on my back. I turned around to find a frantic-looking woman who had apparently pushed her way through the crowd to reach me.

"Yes?" I asked, wondering why she was so anxious to get to me.

"Please, where did you get your leg? My son wants to know where you got it," she blurted.

"Oh," I said. "Here, let's move out of the way of this crowd so I can give you the information."

It was a hot, sunny Saturday afternoon. My wife and I had gone to Costco to pick up our weekly groceries and to see our friend Dave. We had just finished checking out and were merging into the long line of people as they exited the warehouse to get their receipts checked. The woman had pushed her way up to us, her young son in tow.

Kami had seen the little boy earlier by the food court, eating a swirled ice cream treat. She had noticed his rather large shin guards, and figured he had just finished playing a soccer game and had come with his mother to Costco to get a cool treat.

We left the warehouse and moved away from the exit to exchange information.

"My son, he wants to know where you got your leg and who makes your shoes." the woman asked again. She began to explain that her son had a disease, and that his feet had been amputated. She told me about their current prosthetist and the limitations her son had been living with. "His current prosthetics are just so bulky and heavy. We were always told that was all there was, until we saw your leg," she said. "He's only nine years old and just wants to be like other kids and jump on the trampoline and ride his bike." She was almost in tears. The boy was ogling my shiny, carbon graphite leg and checking out my half shoes. He continued working on his ice cream cone, carefully licking the sides clean so he didn't miss a drop. I gave the woman the information for my prosthetist, Mike Pack with Artificial Limb Specialists in Phoenix. She hurriedly typed all the information into her iPad. I talked with her about what I used and how my shoes were made.

Kami leaned down to the little boy, who was still staring up at me in amazement. She said, "I bet you would never guess that he has four gold medals."

"WHAT?" the little boy shouted. "How did he get them?"

"He was a sprinter, he was the fastest man in the world. He held world records."

"WOW!" the little boy's eyes grew huge as he continued staring up at me.

"See, you can do anything you want to if you put your mind to it," Kami told the boy.

"That is what my dad *always* says!" he shouted.

The woman couldn't thank me enough and I could tell she was visibly shaken. My guess is that she was so overwhelmed by the possibility that there *were* actually other types of prosthetics that could help her son, and she was excited to find something that would make him feel more like "the other kids."

My wife and I left the warehouse and started loading the car.

We looked at each other and realized that this was one of those moments—universal "chance" had set it in motion. My life had been full of these types of events, and this would be another time that would be frozen in my mind forever. I was meant to meet that little boy and his mother.

I couldn't help but feel that the child was going to benefit from the information I had given his mom and that just maybe he would be able to ride his bike and jump on the trampoline with the help of new, lighter legs. I saw the spark of determination in his eyes and knew that he would push through his diversity and limitations to achieve whatever he set his mind to. It felt good to know that I was in the right place at the right time for someone else.

Sometimes it takes one person, one voice, one action . . . to set off a chain of events that impacts millions of lives. And of course that had always been my dream, my goal, to show others that, no matter your situation, "If you can dream it, you can achieve it."

After that day at Costco my mind was stirring. Thoughts that had been dormant for several years as a struggling single father, just trying to stay afloat, came boiling to the surface. When I stopped running in 2001, I thought that the days of making a big impact and sharing my message was behind me. After all, I was just a normal guy working a nine to five now. Gone were the days of being in front of the camera, the man without hands or feet breaking world records. But if sharing my message one person at a time, one event at a time, starting a chain reaction was the way I had to do it now, so be it.

When I slept at night, I'd dream of running competitively again. Kami would shake me awake in the middle of the night and ask me if I was okay. Apparently I was shaking the bed, running in my sleep. I had vivid dreams of flying down the track, my arms and legs pumping as fast as they would go, slipping into that high gear and then accelerating across the finish line.

In daylight hours I obsessed about how to pick up where I left off in 2001. Not necessarily with running, but with reaching out to others to act as an example, and to give others hope. How could I still make that impact? I needed to be in the right place at the right time to help others. Was it possible to do that?

I knew that I needed a change. I had been in a limbo of sorts for the last nine years. The more I thought about it, and the more Kami encouraged me to start living my dream again, the more I wanted to get back to my "true self" and share my message with others, as well as regain the mental and physical clarity I had during my peak competition days.

It started off simply enough. I found a gym and got back into shape. Not any gym would do. I had special needs with regard to weightlifting. I needed one-on-one attention and I had to find someone who would help me discover new ways to train, considering my limitations. I had looked around for a while, but the big commercial gyms with monthly memberships weren't for me. I didn't want to be on display.

One day we were driving in a part of town that we frequented. In fact we had driven the road hundreds of times. We saw a sign outside a shopping center that said, "Spartan Training: Give us a try before you hire a personal trainer." We decided to stop in and see what it was all about. We were pleased to find that it was not like the other big nationally franchised gyms. It was locally owned and operated—homegrown.

I met the owner, Robert Leasure, and his wife Vicki. Initially

Robert was hesitant to train me. He had never worked with anyone who didn't have hands or feet. This was a new challenge for him, for sure, but he was more than up to it.

Robert's creativity allowed me to complete exercises that I had never before done in my life! For instance, I'd never done pull ups. Imagine that . . . a man with no hands doing pull ups! But Robert enabled me to do them, along with many other exercises that had seemed impossible for me before I met him. Since I have been with Robert and Spartan Training I have dropped down to 6.09 percent body fat. I wasn't that low even in my competition days.

Several other gym members stopped by during breaks in our workouts to tell me how inspiring I was. They'd say pretty much the same thing: "If you can do it, I should be able to do it, too. It makes me push myself harder when I see how dedicated you are."

Robert was so impressed with my work ethic, he tells clients this about me:

I remember the first day Tony walked into the Spartan Studio. I was very busy with clients and as soon as I could get away, I walked over to Tony and his wife Kami and introduced myself. Almost immediately I realized Tony was a very unique person. We talked for a while about his fitness goals and the strategy for reaching those goals.

Tony presented a unique challenge for me as a personal trainer and I was excited to get started with his training. Since that first day I have gained a lot of insight into training Tony. He is an athlete with a perspective that sees the world through a lens of potential and possibility. I always tell people, when you walk through the door of our studio, "Leave the 'can't' and 'cannot's' outside, because we do not allow 'can't' in this studio." Tony is a standing example to all our clients of this principle. His determination and conviction to achieve and succeed are an inspiration to us all. Tony really gives all of us here at the Spartan Studio a realistic perspective on our own training abilities.

I think the message that we all get from Tony is: Giving 100 percent to life is the ability to achieve victory without perfection. In seeing the perfection within the imperfection, you create a potential for transcending the limitations of the human condition. The vision of a true champion always sees beyond the limitations of the mind, into the powerful possibilities that life presents in the living of it.

The studio displays some great pictures of Spartan warriors going to battle. Tony's picture is among those hanging on the wall.

But exercise wasn't the only thing that started to change. It seems that when you put your intentions out into the universe, and if this path is the one you are meant to follow, fate always leads you in the right direction.

By now, I had been working on my life story and getting myself in shape, but there was more to come.

In July of 2011, I received the following e-mail:

Greetings,

My name is Keith Bryant and I administer the Team USA Ambassador Program for the United States Olympic Committee (USOC). You are receiving this e-mail because you have been identified as a strong ambassador for the United States and Olympic/Paralympic movement by the positive actions you've taken both on and off the field of play. We are requesting your consideration to be an ambassador/facilitator/mentor for the Team USA Ambassador Programs that the USOC will administer to Olympic and Paralympic hopefuls training for the 2012 Olympic Games in London.

The Team USA Ambassador Program was initially created for the 2008 Olympic and Paralympic Teams training for the games in Beijing. It was so successful that the program was implemented again prior to the 2010 Olympic Winter Games in Vancouver and is now a fixture in the preparation of U.S. Olympic and Paralympic Teams in the year leading up to the London games.

I felt so honored that the USOC would consider me for this

opportunity and by the end of August I found myself in Colorado Springs, Colorado, at the U.S. Olympic Training Center, helping to facilitate the first of many Team USA Ambassador Programs.

Not only was I now back in the Olympic world, spreading my message and sharing my experiences from that time in my life, but I was making a real difference by doing so to all those up-and-coming athletes and Olympic hopefuls.

What happened next came as a complete surprise. One day, out of the blue, Keith Bryant called me and said, "Tony, I wanted to be the one to tell you. You have been nominated to be inducted into the Olympic Hall of Fame, Class of 2012." Wow! I was humbled and excited to be chosen as one of the few nominees for this great honor.

> *The U.S. Olympic Hall of Fame was established in 1979 to celebrate the achievements of America's premier athletes in the Modern Olympic Games. The first U.S. Olympic Hall of Fame class was inducted in 1983 during ceremonies in Chicago and included Olympic greats such as Bob Beamon, Cassius Clay, Peggy Fleming, Al Oerter, Jesse Owens, Wilma Rudolph, Mark Spitz, Jim Thorpe and the 1980 "Miracle on Ice" men's ice hockey team.*
>
> *Hall of Fame inductees are selected by the U.S. Olympic Hall of Fame Nominating Committee, U.S. Olympians Association, the Olympic Family and the general public. The 2012 Hall of Fame Induction Ceremony presented by Allstate will be held on July 12 at the Harris Theater in Chicago. The nominee list consisted of 18 individual Olympic athletes, five Paralympic athletes and five teams. (http://www.teamusa.org/About-the-USOC/Hall-of-Fame/2012-Nominees.aspx)*

The inductee selections came from combining public vote totals with Olympians, Paralympians and U.S. Olympic family members to determine the six Olympians, one Paralympian and one team that would make up the Class of 2012.

(As I finish writing my book, the announcement for who has won the honor has yet to be released.) Things were starting to come full circle. It seemed as though that day at Costco had set about a chain of events that would be unstoppable—and I certainly didn't want it to end. Whether I won the nomination or not, I was on this path now and the sky was the limit.

I wanted to reach out to as many people as possible: Individuals who had similar situations to mine; possibly born without a limb, or maybe had an amputation because of an accident, or as the result of military service for our great country. The little boy at Costco had me thinking. *What can I do to be that person who is there to assist? Can I somehow share my knowledge and contacts to give them a greater chance at success?*

That's when it hit me: a foundation for amputees. The organization could offer assistance, aid or grants to those individuals who show a love of life and determination to take control of their fate and pursue their dreams. Maybe it is the girl next door who has no hands, but dreams of painting or playing the piano. Or possibly it is the little boy who wants to ride his bike, or jump on the trampoline, or even become the next great Paralympian. It could be an adult: the war hero who has lost his legs and needs the right tools and prosthetics to allow him to climb Mt. Everest. These are the people that I wanted to reach, to help.

The Helping Others Live Determined Foundation would do just that. It's been a slow start; something like this doesn't happen overnight. Because I'm a big dreamer, I have lofty goals. My vision is to eventually expand this foundation to be able to provide an elite, state-of-the-art training facility to both established Paralympians and promising hopefuls.

It became even more solidified in my heart and mind that this is something I *had* to work toward, when by chance my old coach Bryan Hoddle was in Phoenix for a track meet at Arizona State

University and had been visiting my prosthetist. I got a call one day.

"Hey dreamer, you still living the dream?" said the familiar voice on the phone. It was Bryan. I hadn't seen or spoken to him in thirteen years. The next day we met at ASU, and after the track meet we went to lunch. I introduced Bryan to Kami and we caught up on our lives. Bryan told me that I looked like I was in better shape than ever and in the course of our conversation I felt that spark, that desire, to run again.

The events over the last decade have led me to the place I am now, and what a wonderful place it is. I have so many hopes and have rekindled dreams for the future. I am having a new set of running legs made as I write this. After eleven years off the track, I am ready to get back on it and see what I have left the tank. If nothing else, I'll get back to doing something I have always loved: flying down the track, feeling my heart hammering in my chest, my breath rushing in and out in with a sensation of strength and power, and nothing holding me back . . .

And, imagining that I am, still, the fastest man in the world . . .

APPENDIX

Tony Volpentest's Track Achievements

Track Activities

1989, Pan Am Games for Physically Disabled Youth,
Tampa, Florida

> 60 meters, 1st place, 8.95 seconds
> 100 meters, 1st place, 14.38 seconds
> 200 meters, 1st place, 31.08 seconds

1989, United States Amputee Athletic Association Nationals,
New York, New York

> 100 meters, 1st place (junior division), 14.3 seconds
> 200 meters, 1st place (junior division), 30.5 seconds

1989, World Championships for Disabled Youth/Junior Orange Bowl,
Miami, Florida

> 100 meters, 1st place, 14.1 seconds
> 200 meters, 1st place, 29.5 seconds

1990, World Championships for Disabled Youth,
St. Etienne, France

> 100 meters, 1st place, 13.1 seconds
> 200 meters, 1st place, 27.5 seconds
> 400 meters, 1st place, 66.0 seconds

1990, USAAA National Championships, Bowling Green, Ohio

100 meters, 2nd place (senior division), 12.6 seconds

200 meters, 2nd place (senior division), 26.7 seconds

1991, USA/MOBIL Outdoor Track & Field Championships, New York, New York

100 meters (amputee exhibition race), 1st place, 11.74 seconds (Accutrac), new U. S. record

1991, USODA Victory Games/Paralympic Trials, New York, New York

100 meters, 1st place, 11.65 seconds (wind-aided)
   unofficial world record (official = 11.73 seconds)

200 meters, 1st place, 24.24 seconds (wind-aided)
   unofficial world record (official = 24.36 seconds)

1992, National Handicapped Sports Amputee Games, Atlanta, Georgia

100 meters, 1st place, 11.76 seconds

200 meters, 1st place, 23.70 seconds,
   (new U.S. record)

1992, IX Paralympic Games, Barcelona, Spain

100 meters, 1st place, 11.63 seconds
   (new world record)

200 meters, 1st place 23.07 seconds,
   (new world record)

4x100-meter relay, 2nd place, 45.97 seconds

1996, X Paralympic Games,
Atlanta, Georgia

100 meters, 1st place, 11.36 seconds
(new world record)
200 meters, 1st place, 23.28 seconds

1997, One to One Challenge of Champions,
Toronto, Canada

100 meters, 1st place, 11.69 seconds

1999, ISOD World Championships,
Barcelona, Spain

100 meters, 1st place, 11.39 seconds
200 meters, 1st place, 22.85 seconds
(new world record)

2000, XI Paralympic Games,
Sydney, Australia

100 meters, 4th place, 11.81 seconds
200 meters DNF (Did Not Finish)

Able-Bodied Competition

1991, Edmonds-Woodway Track
(high school)

100 meters, 2nd place, 12.0 seconds
(personal best)
200 meters, 3rd place, 24.6 seconds
(personal best)
Earned varsity letter in high school

1992, West Seattle All-comers Meet (multiple weeks), Seattle, Washington

> 100 meters, 1st place, 11.79 seconds
> 200 meters, 1st place, 23.90 seconds

1993, West Seattle All-comers Meet (multiple weeks), Seattle, Washington

> 100 meters, 1st place, 11.79 seconds
> (season best)
> 200 meters, 1st place, 24.35 seconds
> (season best)

1996, University of Washington All-comers Meet, Seattle, Washington

> 55 meters, 7.35 seconds
> (world indoor best)

1996, Bill Cosby Classic, Reno, Nevada

> 55 meters, 7.19 seconds
> (world indoor best)
> 200 meters, 25.04 seconds
> (world indoor best/banked track)

1996, Simplot Games, Pocatello, Idaho

> 55 meters, 7.19 seconds
> 60 meters, 7.70 seconds
> (world indoor best)
> 200 meters, 1st place, 25.20 seconds

1996, Arcadia Invitational, Arcadia, California

> 100 meters, 1st place, 11.74 seconds
> (-2.76 mps headwind)
> 200 meters, 1st place, 23.70 seconds
> (-2.77 mps headwind)

1996, Phil Long's Run for the Homeless, Colorado Springs, Colorado

> 100 meters, 2nd place, 11.66 seconds
> (-2.50 mps headwind)
> 200 meters, 1st place, 22.67 seconds
> (unofficial world record, -1.50 mps headwind)

1996, Rice University All-comers Meet, Houston, Texas

> 100 meters, 1st place, 10.98 seconds
> (unofficial world record)
> 200 meters, 2nd place, 22.86 seconds

1999, Edmonds All-comers Meet (multiple weeks), Edmonds, Washington

> 100 meters, 1st place,11.81 seconds
> (season best)
> 200 meters, 1st place, 24.12 seconds
> (season best)

About the Author

 Tony Volpentest has been breaking world records and winning Paralympic gold medals since 1992. His numerous awards include the International Olympic Committee Presidents Disabled Athletes Award, the United States Olympic Committee Athlete of the Year Award, and Sports Star of the Year. He served as the National Spokesman for Shriner's Hospitals and has been featured on numerous radio and TV shows, including CNN and *Ripley's Believe It or Not,* and was a *Sports Illustrated* Athlete of the Year. Tony had the great honor of being nominated to be inducted into the Olympic Hall of Fame, Class of 2012.

Tony is married and the father of four children. Through his foundation, Helping Others Live Determined, he works with others who are aspiring to be champions in all aspects of life. He is currently training again, and given his determination and "never give up" attitude, don't be surprised if you see him on the track again soon.

For more information about the Helping Others Live Determined Foundation or to contact Tony visit: *www.tonyvolpentest.com.*

Other Books by
Bettie Youngs Book Publishers

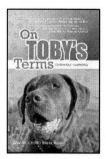

On Toby's Terms

Charmaine Hammond

On Toby's Terms is an endearing story of a beguiling creature who teaches his owners that, despite their trying to teach him how to be the dog they want, he is the one to lay out the terms of being the dog he needs to be. This insight would change their lives forever.

Simply a beautiful book about life, love, and purpose. —**Jack Canfield, compiler,** *Chicken Soup for the Soul* **series**

In a perfect world, every dog would have a home and every home would have a dog like Toby! —**Nina Siemaszko, actress,** *The West Wing*

This is a captivating, heartwarming story and we are very excited about bringing it to film. —**Steve Hudis, Producer**

Soon to be a major motion picture!

ISBN: 978-0-9843081-4-9 • $14.95

Diary of a Beverly Hills Matchmaker

Marla Martenson

Marla takes her readers for a hilarious romp through her days in an exclusive matchmaking agency. From juggling the demands of out-of-touch clients and trying to meet the capricious demands of an insensitive boss to the ups and downs of her own marriage with a husband who doesn't think that she is "domestic" enough, Marla writes with charm and self-effacement about the universal struggles of finding the love of our lives—and knowing it.

Martenson's irresistible quick wit will have you rolling on the floor.
—**Megan Castran, international YouTube Queen**

ISBN: 978-0-9843081-0-1 • $14.95

The Maybelline Story—And the Spirited Family Dynasty Behind It

Sharrie Williams

Throughout the twentieth century, Maybelline inflated, collapsed, endured, and thrived in tandem with the nation's upheavals. Williams, to avoid unwanted scrutiny of his private life, cloistered himself behind the gates of his Rudolph Valentino Villa and ran his empire from a distance. This never before told story celebrates the life of a man whose vision rocketed him to success along with the woman held in his orbit: his brother's wife, Evelyn Boecher—who became his lifelong fascination and muse. A fascinating and inspiring story, a tale both epic and intimate, alive with the clash, the hustle, the music, and dance of American enterprise.

A richly told story of a forty-year, white-hot love triangle that fans the flames of a major worldwide conglomerate. —**Neil Shulman, Associate Producer,** *Doc Hollywood*

Salacious! Engrossing! There are certain stories, so dramatic, so sordid, that they seem positively destined for film; this is one of them. —*New York Post*

ISBN: 978-0-9843081-1-8 • $18.95

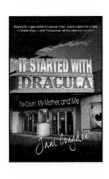

It Started with Dracula

The Count, My Mother, and Me

Jane Congdon

The terrifying legend of Count Dracula silently skulking through the Transylvania night may have terrified generations of filmgoers, but the tall, elegant vampire captivated and electrified a young Jane Congdon, igniting a dream to one day see his mysterious land of ancient castles and misty hollows. Four decades later she finally takes her long-awaited trip—never dreaming that it would unearth decades-buried memories, and trigger a life-changing inner journey. A memoir full of surprises, Jane's story is one of hope, love—and second chances.

Unfinished business can surface when we least expect it. *It Started with Dracula* is the inspiring story of two parallel journeys: one a carefully planned vacation and the other an astonishing and unexpected detour in healing a wounded heart. —**Charles Whitfield, MD, bestselling author of** *Healing the Child Within*

An elegantly written and cleverly told story. An electrifying read. —**Diane Bruno, CISION Media**

ISBN: 978-1-936332-10-6 • $15.95

The Rebirth of Suzzan Blac

Suzzan Blac

A horrific upbringing and then abduction into the sex slave industry would all but kill Suzzan's spirit to live. But a happy marriage and two children brought love—and forty-two stunning paintings, art so raw that it initially frightened even the artist. "I hid the pieces for 15 years," says Suzzan, "but just as with the secrets in this book, I am slowing sneaking them out, one by one by one." Now a renowned artist, her work is exhibited world-wide.

A story of inspiration, truth and victory.

A solid memoir about a life reconstructed. Chilling, thrilling, and thought provoking. —**Pearry Teo, Producer,** *The Gene Generation*

ISBN: 978-1-936332-22-9 • $16.95

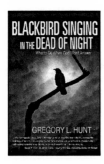

Blackbird Singing in the Dead of Night
What to Do When God Won't Answer

Gregory L. Hunt

Pastor Greg Hunt had devoted nearly thirty years to congregational ministry, helping people experience God and find their way in life. Then came his own crisis of faith and calling. While turning to God for guidance, he finds nothing. Neither his education nor his religious involvements could prepare him for the disorienting impact of the experience.

Alarmed, he tries an experiment. The result is startling—and changes his life entirely.

In this most beautiful memoir, Greg Hunt invites us into an unsettling time in his life, exposes the fault lines of his faith, and describes the path he walked into and out of the dark. Thanks to the trail markers he leaves along the way, he makes it easier for us to find our way, too. —**Susan M. Heim, co-author,** *Chicken Soup for the Soul, Devotional Stories for Women*

Compelling. If you have ever longed to hear God whispering a love song into your life, read this book. —**Gary Chapman,** *NY Times* **bestselling author,** *The Love Languages of God*

ISBN: 978-1-936332-07-6 • $15.95

DON CARINA
WWII Mafia Heroine

Ron Russell

A father's death in Southern Italy in the 1930s—a place where women who can read are considered unfit for marriage—thrusts seventeen-year-old Carina into servitude as a "black widow," a legal head of the household who cares for her twelve siblings. A scandal forces her into a marriage to Russo, the "Prince of Naples."

By cunning force, Carina seizes control of Russo's organization and disguising herself as a man, controls the most powerful of Mafia groups for nearly a decade. Discovery is inevitable: Interpol has been watching. Nevertheless, Carina survives to tell her children her stunning story of strength and survival.

978-0-9843081-9-4 • $15.95

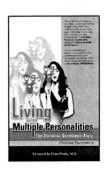

Living with Multiple Personalities
The Christine Ducommun Story

Christine Ducommun

Christine Ducommun was a happily married wife and mother of two, when—after moving back into her childhood home—she began to experience panic attacks and a series of bizarre flashbacks. Eventually diagnosed with Dissociative Identity Disorder (DID), Christine's story details an extraordinary twelve-year ordeal unraveling the buried trauma of her past and the daunting path she must take to heal from it. Therapy helps to identify Christine's personalities and understand how each helped her cope with her childhood, but she'll need to understand their influence on her adult life.

Fully reawakened and present, the personalities compete for control of Christine's mind as she bravely struggles to maintain a stable home for her growing children. In the shadows, her life tailspins into unimaginable chaos—bouts of drinking and drug abuse, sexual escapades, theft and fraud—leaving her to believe she may very well be losing the battle for her sanity. Nearing the point of surrender, a breakthrough brings integration.

A brave story of identity, hope, healing and love.

Reminiscent of the Academy Award-winning *A Beautiful Mind*, this true story will have you on the edge of your seat. Spellbinding! —**Josh Miller, Producer**

ISBN: 978-0-9843081-5-6 • $16.95

Amazing Adventures of a Nobody

Leon Logothetis

Tired of his disconnected life and uninspiring job, Leon leaves it all behind—job, money, home even his cell phone—and hits the road with nothing but the clothes on his back. His journey from Times Square to the Hollywood sign relying on the kindness of strangers and the serendipity of the open road, inspires a dramatic and life changing transformation.

A gem of a book; endearing, engaging and inspiring. —**Catharine Hamm,** *Los Angeles Times* **Travel Editor**

Leon reaches out to every one of us who has ever thought about abandoning our routines and living a life of risk and adventure. His tales of learning to rely on other people are warm, funny, and entertaining. If you're looking to find meaning in this disconnected world of ours, this book contains many clues. —*Psychology Today*

ISBN: 978-0-9843081-3-2 • $14.95

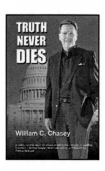

Truth Never Dies

William C. Chasey

A lobbyist for some 40 years, William C. Chasey represented some of the world's most prestigious business clients and twenty-three foreign governments before the US Congress. His integrity never questioned.

All that changed when Chasey was hired to forge communications between Libya and the US Congress. A trip he took with a US Congressman for discussions with then Libyan leader Muammar Qadhafi forever changed Chasey's life. Upon his return, his bank accounts were frozen, clients and friends had been advised not to take his calls.

Things got worse: the CIA, FBI, IRS, and the Federal Judiciary attempted to coerce him into using his unique Libyan access to participate in a CIA-sponsored assassination plot of the two Libyans indicted for the bombing of Pan Am flight 103. Chasey's refusal to cooperate resulted in the destruction of his reputation, a six-year FBI investigation and sting operation, financial ruin, criminal charges, and incarceration in federal prison.

A somber tale, a thrilling read. —**Gary Chafetz, author,** *The Perfect Villain: John McCain and the Demonization of Lobbyist Jack Abramoff*

ISBN: 978-1-936332-46-5 • $24.95

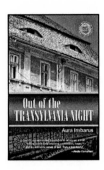

Out of the Transylvania Night

Aura Imbarus

A Pulitzer-Prize entry

"I'd grown up in the land of Transylvania, homeland to Dracula, Vlad the Impaler, and worse, dictator Nicolae Ceausescu," writes the author. "Under his rule, like vampires, we came to life after sundown, hiding our heirloom jewels and documents deep in the earth." Fleeing to the US to rebuild her life, she discovers a startling truth about straddling two cultures and striking a balance between one's dreams and the sacrifices that allow a sense of "home."

Aura's courage shows the degree to which we are all willing to live lives centered on freedom, hope, and an authentic sense of self. Truly a love story!
—**Nadia Comaneci, Olympic Champion**

A stunning account of erasing a past, but not an identity. —**Todd Greenfield, 20th Century Fox**

ISBN: 978-0-9843081-2-5 • $14.95

Universal Co-opetition
Nature's Fusion of
Co-operation and Competition

V Frank Asaro

A key ingredient in business success is competition—and cooperation. Too much of one or the other can erode personal and organizational goals. This book identifies and explains the natural, fundamental law that unifies the apparently opposing forces of cooperation and competition. By finding this synthesis point in a variety of situations—from the personal to the organizational—this is the ultimate recipe for individual or group success.

"Your extraordinary book has given me valuable insights." —**Spencer Johnson, author, *Who Moved My Cheese***

ISBN 978-1-936332-08-3 • $14.95 US

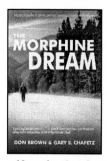

The Morphine Dream

Don Brown with Boston Globe Pulitzer nominated Gary S. Chafetz

At 36, high-school dropout and a failed semi-professional ballplayer Donald Brown hit bottom when an industrial accident left him immobilized. But Brown had a dream while on a morphine drip after surgery: he imagined himself graduating from Harvard Law School (he was a classmate of Barack Omaba) and walking across America. Brown realizes both seemingly unreachable goals, and achieves national recognition as a legal crusader for minority homeowners. This intriguing tale of his long walk—both physical and metaphorical—is an amazing story of loss, gain and the power of perseverance.

"An incredibly inspirational memoir." —**Alan M. Dershowitz, professor, Harvard Law School**

September 2012
ISBN 978-1-936332-25-0 • $16.95 US

Hostage of Paradox: A Memoir

John Rixey Moore

A profound odyssey of a college graduate who enlists in the military to avoid being drafted, becomes a Green Beret Airborne Ranger, and is sent to Vietnam where he is plunged into high-risk, deep-penetration operations under contract to the CIA—work for which he was neither specifically trained nor psychologically prepared, yet for which he is ultimately highly decorated. Moore survives, but can't shake the feeling that some in the military didn't care if he did, or not. Ultimately he would have a 40-year career in television and film.

A compelling story told with extraordinary insight, disconcerting reality, and engaging humor. —**David Hadley, actor, *China Beach***

September 2012
ISBN: 978-1-936332-37-3 • $24.95

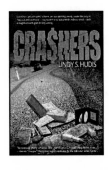

Crashers
A Tale of "Cappers" and "Hammers"

Lindy S. Hudis

The illegal business of fraudulent car accidents is a multi-million dollar racket, involving unscrupulous medical providers, personal injury attorneys, and the cooperating passengers involved in the accidents. Innocent people are often swept into it.

Newly engaged Nathan and Shari, who are swimming in mounting debt, were easy prey: seduced by an offer from a stranger to move from hard times to good times in no time, Shari finds herself the "victim" in a staged auto accident. Shari gets her payday, but breaking free of this dark underworld will take nothing short of a miracle.

A riveting story of love, life—and limits. A non-stop thrill ride. —**Dennis "Danger" Madalone, stunt coordinator for the television series,** *Castle*

ISBN: 978-1-936332-27-4 • $16.95

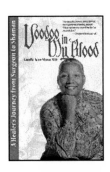

Voodoo in My Blood
A Healer's Journey from Surgeon to Shaman

Carolle Jean-Murat, M.D.

Born and raised in Haiti to a family of healers, US trained physician Carolle Jean-Murat came to be regarded as a world-class surgeon. But her success harbored a secret: in the operating room, she could quickly intuit the root cause of her patient's illness, often times knowing she could help the patient without having to put her under the knife. Carolle knew that to fellow surgeons, her intuition was best left unmentioned. But when the devastating earthquake hit Haiti and Carolle returned to help—she had to acknowledge the shaman she had become.

This mesmerizing story takes us inside the secret world of voodoo as a healing practice, and sheds light on why it remains a mystery to most and shunned by many.

"A beautiful memoir." —**Christiane Northrup, M.D.**

"A masterpiece! Truly enlightening. A personal story you won't soon forget." —**Adrianne Belafonte-Bizemeyer**

October 2012
ISBN 978-1-936332-05-2 • $24.95 US

The Law of Attraction for Teens
How to Get More of the Good Stuff, and Get Rid of the Bad Stuff!

Christopher Combates

Whether it's getting better grades, creating better relationships with your friends, parents, or teachers, or getting a date for the prom, the Law of Attraction just might help you bring it about. It works like this: Like attracts like. When we align our goals with our best intentions and highest purpose, when we focus on what we want, we are more likely to bring it about. This book will help teens learn how to think, act, and communicate in the positive way.

ISBN: 978-1-936332-29-8 • $14.95

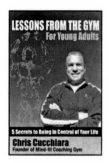

Lessons from the Gym for Young Adults
5 Secrets to Being in Control of Your Life

Chris Cucchiara

Do you lack self-confidence or have a difficult time making decisions? Do you ever have a tough time feeling a sense of purpose and belonging? Do you worry that you don't measure up? Or that you're doing what other people want of you, instead of what you want?

Growing up, Chris Cucchiara felt the same, until he joined a gym. The lessons he learned helped him gain the confidence he needed to set and achieve goals. In *Lessons from the Gym for Yourg Adults*, Chris shares his experiences and powerful insights and shows you how to:

- develop mental toughness (a life without fear, stress, and anger);
- develop an attitude to get and stay healthy and fit;
- build an "athlete for life" mentality that stresses leadership and excellence as a mindset; and,
- stay motivated, and set and achieve goals that matter.

ISBN 978-1-936332-38-0 • $14.95 US

In bookstores everywhere, online, Espresso,
or from the publisher, Bettie Youngs Books:

www.BettieYoungsBooks.com

To contact:
info@BettieYoungsBooks.com

Bettie Youngs Books

We specialize in MEMOIRS
. . . books that celebrate
fascinating people and
remarkable journeys

VISIT OUR WEBSITE AT
www.BettieYoungsBooks.com